THE HOME PLACE

THE HOME PLACE

Memoirs of a Colored Man's Love Affair with Nature

J. Drew Lanham

milkweed
editions

Published 2016 by Milkweed Editions
Printed in the United States of America
Cover design by Mary Austin Speaker
Cover photo of Carolina wren by
Stephen Tabone Nature Photography / NatureExposures.com
Author photo by D. Colby Lanham
16 17 18 19 20   5 4 3 2 1
First Edition

Special underwriting for this book was contributed by the Hlavka family.

Milkweed Editions, an independent nonprofit publisher, gratefully acknowledges sustaining support from the Jerome Foundation; the Lindquist & Vennum Foundation; the McKnight Foundation; the National Endowment for the Arts; the Target Foundation; and other generous contributions from foundations, corporations, and individuals. Also, this activity is made possible by the voters of Minnesota through a Minnesota State Arts Board Operating Support grant, thanks to a legislative appropriation from the arts and cultural heritage fund, and a grant from the Wells Fargo Foundation Minnesota. For a full listing of Milkweed Editions supporters, please visit www.milkweed.org.

Library of Congress Cataloging-in-Publication Data

Names: Lanham, J. Drew (Joseph Drew), author.
Title: The home place : memoirs of a colored man's love affair with nature / J. Drew Lanham.
Description: First edition. | Minneapolis, Minnesota : Milkweed Editions, 2016.
Identifiers: LCCN 2016009677 (print) | LCCN 2016024050 (ebook) | ISBN 9781571313157 (hardcover : alk. paper) | ISBN 9781571318756 (e-book)
Subjects: LCSH: Lanham, J. Drew (Joseph Drew) | Zoologists--South Carolina--Biography. | African American zoologists--South Carolina--Biography. | Conservationists--South Carolina--Biography. | African American conservationists--South Carolina--Biography.
Classification: LCC QL31.L373 A3 2016 (print) | LCC QL31.L373 (ebook) | DDC 590.92 [B] --dc23
LC record available at https://lccn.loc.gov/2016009677

Milkweed Editions is committed to ecological stewardship. We strive to align our book production practices with this principle, and to reduce the impact of our operations in the environment. We are a member of the Green Press Initiative, a nonprofit coalition of publishers, manufacturers, and authors working to protect the world's endangered forests and conserve natural resources. *The Home Place* was printed on acid-free 100% postconsumer-waste paper by Edwards Brothers Malloy.

For all who wander and love the land

Contents

THE HOME PLACE

Me: An Introduction

> I prefer to be true to myself, even at the hazard of incur-
> ring the ridicule of others, rather than to be false, and
> incur my own abhorrence.
>
> —Frederick Douglass,
> *Narrative of the Life of Frederick Douglass*

I AM A MAN IN LOVE WITH NATURE. I AM AN ECO-ADDICT,
consuming everything that the outdoors offers in its all-you-can-
sense, seasonal buffet. I am a wildling, born of forests and fields
and more comfortable on unpaved back roads and winding woodland paths than in any place where concrete, asphalt, and crowds
prevail. In my obsession I "celebrate myself, and sing myself," living Walt Whitman's exaltations, rolling and reveling in all that
nature lays before me.

I am an ornithologist, wildlife ecologist, and college professor.
I am a father, husband, son, and brother. I hope to some I am a
friend. I bird. I hunt. I gather. I am a seeker and a noticer. I am a
lover. My being finds its foundation in open places.

I'm a man of color—African American by politically correct
convention—mostly black by virtue of ancestors who trod ground
in central and west Africa before being brought to foreign shores. In
me there's additionally an inkling of Irish, a bit of Brit, a smidgen of
Scandinavian, and some American Indian, Asian, and Neanderthal
tossed in, too. But that's only a part of the whole: There is also the
red of miry clay, plowed up and planted to pass a legacy forward.

There is the brown of spring floods rushing over a Savannah River shoal. There is the gold of ripening tobacco drying in the heat of summer's last breath. There are endless rows of cotton's cloudy white. My plumage is a kaleidoscopic rainbow of an eternal hope and the deepest blue of despair and darkness. All of these hues are me; I am, in the deepest sense, colored.

I am as much a scientist as I am a black man; my skin defines me no more than my heart does. But somehow my color often casts my love affair with nature in shadow. Being who and what I am doesn't fit the common calculus. I am the rare bird, the oddity: appreciated by some for my different perspective and discounted by others as an unnecessary nuisance, an unusually colored fish out of water.

But in all my time wandering I've yet to have a wild creature question my identity. Not a single cardinal or ovenbird has ever paused in dawnsong declaration to ask the reason for my being. White-tailed deer seem just as put off by my hunter friend's whiteness as they are by my blackness. Responses in forests and fields are not born of any preconceived notions of what "should be." They lie only in the fact that I *am*.

Each of us is so much more than the pigment that orders us into convenient compartments of occupation, avocation, or behavior. It's easy to default to expectation. But nature shows me a better, wilder way. I resist the easy path and claim the implausible, indecipherable, and unconventional.

What is wildness? To be wild is to be colorful, and in the claims of colorfulness there's an embracing and a self-acceptance. We scientists are trained to be comfortable with the multiple questions that each new revelation may elicit. Like sweetgum trees, which find a way to survive in the face of every attempt to exclude them, the questions we ask are persistent resprouts, largely uncontrollable. There really aren't hard-and-fast answers to *most* questions, though. Wildness means living in the unknown. Time is teaching me to extend the philosophies of science to life, to accept the mystery and embrace the next query as an opportunity for another quest.

I find solace, inspiration, and exhilaration in nature. Issues there are boiled down to the simplest imperative: survive. Sometimes my existence seems to hang in the balance of challenges professional and personal, external and internal. What allows me to survive day to day is having nature as my guide.

But I worry as the survival of many of the wild things and places themselves seems increasingly uncertain. Called by something deep inside, I have joined with kindred wandering-wondering watchers and ecologically enlightened spirits in the mission to keep things whole. After all my years of being the scientist–idea generator–objective data gatherer, I yearn for more than statistical explanations.

My colleagues and I have mostly done a poor job of reaching the hearts and minds of those who don't hold advanced degrees with an "ology" at the end. We take a multidimensional array of creatures, places, and interwoven lives and boil them down into the flat pages and prose of obscure journals most will never read. Those tomes are important—but the sin is in leaving the words to die there, pressed between the pages. As knowledge molders in the stacks the public goes on largely uninformed about the wild beings and places that should matter to all of us.

Science's tendency to make the miraculous mundane is like replacing the richest artistry with paint-by-number portraits. In the current climate of scientific sausage making—grinding data through complex statistical packages and then encasing it in a model that often has little chance of real-world implementation—we are losing touch. How inspiring is the output that prescribes some impossible task? How practical is it? We must rediscover the art in conservation and reorient toward doing and not talking.

⌒

What do I live for? I eventually realized that to make a difference I had to step outside, into creation, and refocus on the roots of my passion. If an ounce of soil, a sparrow, or an acre of forest is to remain then we must all push things forward. To save wildlife and wild places the traction has to come not from the regurgitation of bad-news data but from the poets, prophets, preachers, professors, and presidents who have always dared to inspire. Heart and mind cannot be exclusive of one another in the fight to save anything. To help others understand nature is to make it breathe like some giant: a revolving, evolving, celestial being with ecosystems acting as organs and the living things within those places—humans included—as cells vital to its survival. My hope is that somehow I might move others to find themselves magnified in nature, whomever and wherever they might be.

⌒

These chapters are a cataloging of some of the people, places, and things that have shaped me. They are patchwork pieces stitched together by memory. They pose questions: Where do I come from? Who are my people? Why does my blood run wild? These questions and so many more fly like dandelion fluff before me. Each one is a part of some greater whole but seems to have its own destiny. The seeds that find fertile ground yield occasional answers, which eventually send other questions into the breeze. But in the quilt that unfolds I hope I've captured what it took for a bird of a different feather to hatch, fledge, and take flight.

This is a memoir, then, but it is also the story of an ecosystem—of some land, the lives lived on it, and the dreams that unfolded there. It is a tale of an in-between place and its in-between people. And I tell it with a sense of responsibility. I believe the best way to begin reconnecting humanity's heart, mind, and soul to nature is for us to share our individual stories. This is my contribution to that greater mission; sometimes the words that make the fragmented more whole need to come from someone in a different skin. Beyond that, however, I simply hope those words inspire you, too, to see yourself colored in nature's hues.

Flock

The Home Place

Home is a place we all must find, child. It's not just a
place where you eat or sleep. Home is knowing.

⟶ *The Wiz*

IT WAS HOME: EDGEFIELD, SOUTH CAROLINA, A SMALL COUNTY
on the western edge of the Palmetto State. The county's name is
well earned. With its western flank tucked tightly against the banks
of the once mighty but now dammed Savannah River, on the edge
ecologically between Upstate and the Lowcountry, Edgefield con-
tains an incredible natural wealth of mountain, piedmont, and
coastal plain.

Among South Carolina's forty-six counties, Edgefield is not
large, covering only some five hundred square miles. The political boundaries drawn by human hands give it the appearance on
maps of a cartoonish chicken's head, its squared-off comb to the
north, huge triangular beak pointing east toward the Atlantic,
and shortened neck jutting to the southwest. Nature sketched
the westward boundary where Stevens and Turkey Creeks skirt
along the raggedy rear of the bird's head and form the long bor-
der with McCormick County. Surrounded by piedmont places to
the north—Greenwood, McCormick, and Saluda—and Aiken, an
upper–coastal plain county to the south, Edgefield is a transition
zone, with each of the imaginary poultry's portions harboring ecological treasures. Growing up near the bird's scrawny neck—in
the south-central part of the county, only a few miles from the

Savannah River and an equidistant stone's throw from the sprawl
of North Augusta and the sleepy town of Edgefield—I was privy to
the beauty and diversity of a spot most ignore.

Edgefield is many places rolled into one. With the exception
of saltwater and high peaks, there's not much that can't be found
there. Droughty sand holds onto remnant stands of longleaf pine
and stunted turkey oaks in the southern and eastern extremes
where the upper coastal plain peters out. In the soggy bottoms
along many of the rivers and creeks, rich alluvial soils grow
splotchy-barked sycamores and warty hackberries to girths so big
that two large men joined hand to hand couldn't reach around
them. A few buttressed bald cypresses draped in Spanish moss
sit in tea-stained sloughs. Between the extremes of wet and dry,
high and low, even the sticky clay nourishes a surprising variety of
hardwoods; slow-growing upland oaks and tight-grained, tough-
as-nail hickories grow alongside fast-rising tulip poplars and oppor-
tunistic sweetgum. In the understory redbud and dogwood trees
sit in the shade of the dominants, blooming briefly in spring before
the canopy closes with green overhead.

Loblolly pine, the sylvan savior of southern soil, is everywhere. A tree that grows best in moist bottomlands, it climbed the
hills out of the swamps with some help from human hands and
colonized eroding lands. Loblolly is a fast grower that stretches
tall and mostly straight in forests that have been touched occasionally by fire and saw. In open stands, where the widely spaced
trees can grow with broom sedge and Indian grass waving underneath, bobwhite quail, Bachman's sparrows, and a bevy of other
wildlife can find a place to call home. But where flames and forestry have been excluded, spindly trees fight with one another for
sun and soil and will grow thick like the hair on a dog's back.

In those impenetrable stands white-tailed deer find secure bedrooms but little else dwells.

Most of the county sits in the lower piedmont. This Midlands province stretches like a belt, canted southwest to northeast, across the state's thickened waist. Torn apart first by agriculture, then by unbridled development, the fragmented middle sits between the more spectacular coastal plain and the mountains.

Coastward, you'll find black-water swamps, brackish marshes, and disappearing cathedrals of longleaf pine that hide species both common and rare. Red-cockaded woodpeckers, diamondback rattlesnakes, and gopher tortoises hang on in some places where the longleaf persists. Painted buntings splash color across the coastal scrub and alligators bellow in rebounded numbers among wading wood storks.

Northward, the modest Southern Appalachians are bounded by the escarpment the Cherokee called the "Blue Wall." The place not so long ago called the "Dark Corner" still stirs the imagination as gorges rush wild and cool with white water and a few persistent brook trout linger in hidden pools. Moist coves crowded with canopies of hardwoods sit below and among a few granite monoliths that folks flock to see. Within the memory of a three-hundred-year-old poplar this was the backcountry: a wilderness with "panthers," elk, and wood bison roaming canebrakes and rhododendron hells. Now peregrine falcons and common ravens patrol the skies while black bears grow fat on Allegheny blackberries and the easy pickings in exclusive gated communities.

Sitting on either flank of the broad and broken piedmont, the mountains and the coast harbor opportunities for wildness that the worn-out region in between has lost to easy progress. But Edgefield County, caught in the middle of all the apparent mediocrity of the piedmont, is yet a hidden gem, a source of biodiversity that is easy to pass by on the way to somewhere else.

⌒

There are still priceless places where nature hangs on by tooth, talon, and tendril. Most of Edgefield is rural. There are trees everywhere, though most of them reside on private lands, where there is a priority set on pines over pavement. Significant portions of the Sumter National Forest's Long Cane Ranger District lie in the county, providing public access to places where nature is the first consideration. Farming and forestry provide diversity within the tree-dominated matrix. I grew up in the southwestern outreaches of the county, in a ragged, two-hundred-acre Forest Service inholding. From heaven— or from a high-flying bird's viewpoint—I imagine it looked like a hole punched into the Long Cane Ranger District. That gap in the wildness was my Home Place.

In the 1970s, when wild turkeys were still trying to establish a clawhold everywhere else, they were common enough on the Home Place as to be almost unremarkable. I'd often surprise a flock as they fed in the bottomland pasture. Most of the big birds would take off running for the nearest wood's edge, but a couple of gobblers always lifted off, powerfully clearing the tree line while cackling loudly at my intrusion.

Like the wild turkeys, deer weren't really common in the wider world. But whitetails were abundant in the woods and fields of the Home Place. To Daddy, they were pests. Handsome in their foxy red coats, the deer claimed our bean fields as their own in the summer. They seemed to know that there was security in that season, with worries of hidden hunters forgotten until fall.

Daddy put many of the Home Place acres to work growing produce. Watermelon, cantaloupe, butter beans, purple-hull peas, and an array of other crops grew fast and flavorful on the bottom-land terraces and sandy soil up on the hills. Tons of melons and hundreds of bushels of beans were the product of his and Mama's hard work. The bounty wasn't just for us, though. Daddy would load up his truck with the fresh vegetables and sell them to city and suburban folks who craved the flavor of locally grown foods not found in grocery stores. The money was an important supplement to the paltry pay he and Mama made as schoolteachers.

The investment in the crops—the plowing, planting, and fertilizing—would all be for naught, though, if the four-legged foraging machines had their way. The garden's only chance at survival was an eight-foot-high electric fence and a phalanx of scarecrows draped in Daddy's sweatiest, smelliest clothes. Should the fence fail and the deer's noses unriddle the scarecrow ruse, the last line of defense was an old British Enfield .303 rifle. Daddy would sit on the roof and try to pick off one or two of the deer but he was seldom successful. Even with his constant attention to defending the garden he'd often find a sizable portion of the new crop gone overnight, the tender seedlings neatly nipped and ruminating in the belly of a whitetail that had figured out how to breach the gauntlet while we slept.

Knowing that the Home Place was surrounded by the deer heaven of the National Forest and that our fields and gardens were open buffets in the midst of it all, a couple of Daddy's teacher friends—Mr. Sharpe and Mr. Ferguson—asked to hunt the property. Beyond the rooftop plinking Daddy didn't deer hunt, but he believed that any pressure exerted on the bean eaters couldn't hurt. He said yes. The two white men became the only people I remember Daddy ever trusting to hunt on the Home Place, free to roam the property and exact the revenge that my father couldn't. Mr. Sharpe and Mr. Ferguson showed up on Saturday mornings in fall dressed in camouflage and carrying bows or rifles. They sought the whitetails with a dawn-to-dusk fervor, arriving early and leaving late. What did they do out there all day? Where did they go? It was puzzling to see the extraordinary lengths they took—getting up before the sun did and dressing like trees and bushes—just to pursue animals that grazed casually, like so many slender brown cattle, right in our backyard. It seemed to me the hunters were making something that should've been easy hard. But while I don't remember ever seeing any fruits of their labors, they kept coming back and seemed happy just to be "out there."

Beyond the white-tailed deer and the wild turkeys, wildlife was everywhere. In every natural nook and cranny—a stump hole, a dry creek bed, or a burrow in the ground—there was something furred, feathered, finned, or scaled that scurried, swam, or flew. I was amazed by it all. Curiosity grew as I explored and learned the signs of the wild souls I seldom actually saw: the delicate doglike trace of a fox; the handlike pawprints of raccoons and opossums; mysterious feathers that had floated to earth, gifts from unknown birds.

I craved knowledge about the wildlife that lived around us. I read every book I could about the creatures that shared the Home Place kingdom with me. I pored over encyclopedias and piled up library fines. Field guides were treasure troves of information: pictures stacked side by side with brief descriptions of what, where, and when. I went back outdoors, where I walked, stalked, and waited to see as many wild things as I could. I collected tadpoles to watch them grow into froglets; I caught butterflies and gazed into their thousand-lensed eyes. Birds were everywhere and as I learned to identify them by sight their songs sunk into my psyche, too. Nature was often the first and last thing on my mind, morning to night.

An April morning full of birdsong and the distant rumblings of gobbling longbeards was life in stereo. Bobwhite quail had conversations with one another from weedy ditches and thorny thickets. On my rambles I would usually flush a covey or two. The birds exploded from blackberry brambles, flying scattershot in every direction with wings a-whirring, to find refuge elsewhere. The sudden flurry never failed to push my pulse to pounding. Within a few minutes the reassembly calls—*Pearlie! Pearlie!*—drifted across the pasture to bring the clan back together again. On warm summer nights, barred owls boomed their eerie calls and cackles back and forth across the creek bottom as the numbing chants of whip-poor-wills and choruses of katydids and crickets lulled me to sleep.

Today, Edgefield is still a rich refuge for wild things. Most of them don't attract the attention that deer and turkeys do. Hand-standing spotted skunks secret themselves in hedgerows and old fields. Webster's salamanders hide in the litter of the forest floor. Christmas darters, Carolina heelsplitters, yellow lampmussels, and eastern creekshells won't win any contests for charisma but the decorative little fish and trio of freshwater mussels survive in Edgefield's creeks and not many other places. Many rare plants are found there, too. These rooted and leafed things are more often than not overlooked even though their lyrical names demand attention: adder's tongue, streambank mock orange, shoals spider-lily, yellow sunnybell, Oglethorpe oak, eared goldenrod, Carolina birds-in-a-nest, small skullcap, and enchanter's nightshade.

Edgefield has been less welcoming of—and less of a refuge for—human diversity. Under regressive and racist governors who fostered and promoted policies aimed squarely at exclusion and violence, the power base in Edgefield kept things stuck in a state of antebellum stagnation, separate and nowhere near equal. While the South has long laid claim to a culture that values manners, loyalty, honor, and a slower pace of living, there are other, less admirable traits that ooze out from between the niceties. A heaping of hypocrisy is often served alongside the southern hospitality. Double standards are as common as ragweed and persistent as kudzu across the region. The "good old days" that some pine for weren't the best for all of us. But Edgefield was still my refuge, primarily because it was and is a sanctuary for creatures that aren't subject to the prejudices of men.

My memory continues to run like a rabbit around the times spent in the small piedmont place I called home. It weaves and winds through woods and wetlands to reconnect me to my nature-loving roots. That pleasant wandering is reason enough for remembering— and returning—home.

A rusting, dented black mailbox teetering atop a decaying post marked the spot: Route 1, Box 29, Republican Road. Driving west you bore left at the mailbox, onto the dusty dirt road where the county had abandoned regular maintenance to chance and persistent complaints. If you stayed straight on that road for about a quarter of a mile, you'd see a brick house, tinted somewhere between orange and red, the hue of sun-faded clay. The Ranch was a typical 1970s dwelling, nothing spectacular, but mostly modern. It was comfortable and a place Daddy and Mama had worked hard to build. It had been a much smaller house until my parents bought an old army barracks and attached it to the little four-room affair that had been the Lanham abode. They encased the new addition in these clay-colored bricks, added a touch of distinction with white columns on the front porch, and called it home.

The porch looked out over a yard Mama had tried to cover with a slow-growing patch of carpetlike Zoysia grass. But it never lived up to her expectations, and weeds and Bermuda grass had to suffice for lawn. Behind the Ranch a huge hay shed sheltered food for the cattle, Daddy's farm equipment, and almost everything else he thought might be of some future use. There was a chicken coop in the corner of the shed, and on the far side and out of sight (but not smell) a pigpen.

All of it—the Ranch, the hay shed with its tacked-on animal pens—was surrounded by nature. Well-tended gardens, crop fields, and rolling pastures buffered the Home Place from the government timberland. There was even a wetland of sorts, which in later years I would learn was really an open cesspool—the Ranch's own home-made sewage system.

The homestead was also buffered from the outside world. Mama and Daddy were progressive thirtysomethings who'd come through the 1960s civil rights movement. They were still over-coming discrimination but saw a way to provide better for all of us, improving and enlarging their condition. Inside the Ranch there were the decorative signs of 1970s progress: faux-wood paneling and sculpted carpeting in gaudy colors. My big brother, Jock; older sister, Julia ("Bug"); and little sister, Jennifer, all grew up there. For me, though, it was mostly a part-time home. A good portion of my life up until I was fifteen was spent at the other, less-than-modern house that sat across the pasture.

That house—the Ramshackle—was down another road in both

space and time. My grandmother Mamatha's place was everything the brick Ranch wasn't. It had a rusting (and leaky) tin roof, six tiny rooms, and an exterior of brittle, white tiles that were loose or missing in places. The house had a snaggletoothed look where the black tar paper showed through the gapped tile teeth. The porch roof had a ragged hole where she'd shot blindly one night at a hooting owl she claimed was a bad omen.

The yard was Mamatha's pride and joy. She would sit on the wood-planked front porch on warm spring days, admiring her green-thumbed handiwork. Over her five or six decades of occupancy she'd collected fieldstones of every shape and size and arranged them carefully around a huge arborvitae tree. In that dedicated space Mamatha planted all kinds of flowers, which flourished under her constant care. Much of her success depended on the tons of manure she constantly mined from our feedlot. My grandmother worked hard to control things in that little world of stone and cowshit—watering, hoeing, and weeding were neverending work.

Outside the flower ring, however, an army of weeds crept in from the adjoining pasture. Most of what was in that tiny space was green, and from a distance looked lawn-like. There were three or four old crepe myrtles in the yard that erupted in purple and white blooms in April and May. Little copses of lemon-yellow daffodils and nodding snowdrops preceded the crepe myrtles in the new warmth of March. The last time I visited the Home Place many of those flowers, now probably a hundred years old, were still heralding spring.

In the complimentary light of a fading sunset, with your eyes squinted just so, Mamatha's place looked quaint: the little house in the big woods. Coming closer and stepping through the ill-fitting door would reveal the truth, though. Probably built sometime in the 1920s or 1930s, the Ramshackle was almost a functional museum of the Depression-era South. The house was a shoddily constructed thing, with an interior of hastily painted Sheetrock walls and creaky, uneven floors covered by sheets of cheap, fading vinyl. In one room, a remnant piece of threadbare beige carpet provided the "luxurious" touch to an otherwise basic decor. The indoor plumbing, with exposed metal pipes and white enamel basins, was a relatively recent addition. Insulation had been an afterthought. The modern improvements included a 1950s Frigidaire that Mamatha always called an "icebox."

In a scary, dimly lit, and moldy-smelling lower room that had probably been someone's quick-fix idea of an addition, a coffin-sized deep freezer sat entombed in piles of old clothes, magazines, and other junk my pack rat grandmother just couldn't bear to throw away. The freezer kept other items in an icy state of suspended animation. Plastic containers and bags filled with the bounty from gardens past sat stacked and frozen against some future famine. Foil-wrapped mystery meats and leftovers from long-ago church suppers were wedged into every nook and cranny. There was food in there that had seen several decades pass. If Mamatha had pulled a coelacanth—the prehistorically creepy, bottom-dwelling fossil-fish-amphibian—from the depths of that freezer, it wouldn't have been a surprise. I suppose my father came by his hoarding gene honestly.

In spite of her "collecting" my grandmother kept a clean—if not neat—home. Twine-bound brooms made of the tawny stems and tassels of dead broom sedge kept the floors cleaner than any vacuum ever could. Mamatha scrubbed her floors—sometimes on her knees—and seemed always in some mopping, sweeping, or dusting mode.

My grandmother's humble Ramshackle sat next to a dilapi-
dated smokehouse. A notched-log structure that may have been
built decades before the house itself was, it always seemed ready to
give up the ghost to time and gravity. Though salt-cured pork had
hung there in the past, by the time I came along the smokehouse
was a dark and dank junk shed filled with all kinds of unappetiz-
ing and inedible things. My grandfather's World War I gas mask
stared out of the dim like some alien. Cloudy mason jars with God
knows what in them and disintegrating old textbooks and magazines littered the interior. In spite of the eerie aura that surrounded
the shed, I ventured inside occasionally when I was a kid, just to see
what was in there. I never stayed for long and always felt like there
was something lurking in one of the dark corners that I didn't really
want to see.

Mamatha's backyard, mostly compacted dirt with scattered
islands of weeds, struggled even more than the front. There was
a woodpile that waxed and waned with the seasons. A barn with
warped split-board siding had seen its better days twenty or thirty
years before I arrived on the scene. You could see through the siding. The tin roof barely hung onto the rafters. It was a quarrel-
some structure that complained in the slightest wind, creaking
and groaning as if afflicted by some sort of architectural arthritis. Daddy built an elevated corncrib on one side of the barn to
store feed and hay. On the other side was a scrapyard museum of
antiquated junk and artifacts: rusting plowshares, old singletrees,
worn leather harnesses, a burlap sack full of mostly broken arrowheads and pottery made by the people who used to call the same
land *their* home place. The arrowheads were a constant source of
curiosity to me, and I used to wonder about the people ingenious
enough to make such beautiful tools from stone and clay. There was

enough other stuff to keep a kid—or plundering picker—searching
for an eternity. The rickety building was full of the melding odors
of an old farm; the metallic musk of rusting iron and fertilizer,
slick scent of spilled oil, and pleasant aroma of dried corn husks
and molasses-soaked sweet feed mingled with the heavy mustiness
of everything else, from unknown chemicals to toxic pest-killing
potions long ago soaked up by the dirt floor.

There was a barely standing chicken coop behind the barn,
under a gnarled black walnut tree where the hawks would wait for
a chance at chicken dinner. The Ramshackle, the smokehouse, and
the potluck-landscape yard could have all been in a sepia-toned
picture taken long ago. Although my father frequently offered modern upgrades to Mamatha's house and existence, she either filibus-
tered the improvements or downright refused the charity.

There is still a part of me that exists in that tin-roofed,
broomstraw-swept, rusting, rural, wood-fired world. But how did
I, a child of the 1960s and 1970s, come to grow up in the 1930s?
It was all a matter of give and take: I was "loaned" to Mamatha
by Mama and Daddy to help fend off her loneliness after my
grandfather Daddy Joe died in 1961, from a suite of long-lasting
illnesses dating back to World War I. I was, after all, his namesake and thus the most logical substitute; she lost one Joseph and
gained another. So from the age of maybe three or four until I was
sixteen, Mamatha's house was more often home to me than the
Ranch. The two dwellings, the modern and the throwback, sat a
few hundred yards apart from each other, well within hollering
distance. But while the two structures were close together physically they were almost a century apart in mindset. The houses,
and the space that lay between, were symbolic of the worlds I
straddled: modern convenience and comfort versus old-time,

bare-boned simplicity. Both sets of values will guide me until the day I die.

Mamatha's house, broken down and mired in the past like an old plow mule in the mud, was the heart of the Home Place. There was in the antiquated lifestyle something solid and reassuring that comfort and the technology of the day couldn't capture. The ties to legacy and the affection for home were reinforced by a grandmother who, in the "dawning of the Age of Aquarius," somehow kept me suspended in an in-between world of superstitions, haints, and herbal remedies. Any number of apparently innocent things, I learned, might bring bad luck upon me. There were constant warnings—"Don't step over this!" "Don't lay that there!" Mamatha's yard was a walk-through pharmacy, with many of the weeds and roots providing what she claimed the drugstore couldn't. A constant dose of the Holy Bible mixed with magic made my time with my grandmother spooky and spiritually profound.

And so more than the physical structure of the house itself, there was a metaphysical underpinning that defined the character of our lives together. I heard, saw, and felt things in the Ramshackle that few, if any, of my friends have probably ever experienced. It was a universe where wonder and awe had yet to be tossed from the temple by science and cynicism. There was way more to heaven and earth than could be dreamed back then. It was a different world, one I sometimes wish I could revisit.

⌒

There are certain seasons, certain sensual prompts, that take me back to the Home Place. Now, as back then, fall is the time when nature speaks most clearly to me. In autumn one is treated to an orgy of sights, sounds, and smells that can be wonderfully over-whelming. The stifling late-summer heat is mercifully cleared by cooler air overnight. Breathing is suddenly easier and the soak-ing sweat evaporates. You want to inhale deeply enough to take in every molecule wafting on the wind. The tired sameness of September's deep green fades then flames into October's vermil-ion sumacs and scarlet maples, lemon-yellow poplars and golden hickories. In those days of crispness I want to linger long enough to hear every sound and look far enough to see into forever.

The season has always drawn a sort of restlessness from me. The Germans have a fine word for it: *zugunruhe*. A compound derived from the roots *zug* (migration) and *unruhe* (anxiety), it describes the seasonal migration of birds and other animals. In this wanderlust I want to go somewhere far away, to fly to some place I think I need to be. Nature is on the move, too, migrating, stor-ing, and dying. Everything is either accelerating or slowing down. Some things are rushing about to put in seed for the next gener-ation. A monarch butterfly in a field full of goldenrod is urgent on tissue-thin wings of black and orange to gather the surging sweetness before the frost locks it away. Apple trees and tangles of muscadines hang heavy. The fruit-dense orchards offer a final call to the wildlings. Foxes, deer, coons, possum, and wild turkeys fatten in the feasting. The air is spiced with the scent of dying leaves. The perfume of decay gathers as berries ripen into wild wine. Even the sun sits differently in an autumnal sky, sending a mellower light in somber slants that foretell the coming change.

The droning katydids, tired from their months-long work of filling the hot wet nights with song, hang on into October. But soon choirs of thousands dwindle to hundreds, and then just one or two. A persistent cricket tries hard to fiddle in time but the first freeze throws a wrench into his rhythm. The rustling riot of turning, falling leaves and the mysterious moonlit chirps of migrant songbirds winging their way to faraway places make my heart race. It is all so beautiful that it hurts. Almost overnight eastern red cedars suffer the savagery of hormonal surges and a ravaged stand of sapling pines point the way to the pawed-up and piss-soaked patches of ground that whitetail bucks leave as calling cards. When the moon glows in a mid-November sky like a pallid sun, I, too, am so soaked in wanting and wood's lust that I might as well wander like a warbler in the joyous urgency of it all.

~

In Mamatha's bedroom, I slept on an anemic aluminum cot just across from her high-post cannonball bed. For almost a dozen years I tossed and turned on a thin foam mattress that didn't offer much in the way of comfort or support. The cot wobbled and creaked with each move I made. And as I got bigger it got smaller. There was a perfectly good bed in the adjoining room but Mamatha guarded the "guest" bedroom ferociously, keeping it made up in her best linens in a state of museum-like readiness for the company that hardly ever came.

The conservationist prophet Aldo Leopold once wrote, "There are two spiritual dangers in not owning a farm. One is the danger of supposing that breakfast comes from the grocery, and the other that heat comes from the furnace." If the maxim is true then I suppose we were spiritually secure on both counts. Mamatha cooked and heated with wood, not power-company watts. She was always cold, despite sleeping under several suffocating layers of heavy, hand-sewn quilts for most of the year. Even though the bedroom and kitchen were the only heated rooms, the demand for firewood never ended. A ravenous wood heater had a fire in its belly well before the first frost and wasn't extinguished until sometime after Good Friday. In all my years at the Ramshackle that heater probably consumed hundreds of cords of the hardwood that Daddy cut. Thanks to the heater's insatiable appetite and Mamatha's thin blood, the little room could get hellishly hot.

Daddy's wielding of an often finicky chain saw and his choice of the next tree destined for the stove and heater were more art than science. A dying post oak on one hillside or a blown-down poplar from the bottom meant that no stand of timber was ever depleted. He never cut pines for the woodstove because the pitch created a dangerous residue in the flues that could ignite and burn the house down. But the fat lightwood we got from old pine stumps was a coveted commodity and we used it sparingly to start fires. The sap-soaked heartwood smelled like kerosene and burned like a torch.

In addition to the firewood gathered for Mamatha, the forest freely sacrificed sturdy posts and rails of hickory for corrals and fences. Big sweetgum and elm trees were left standing because they were almost impossible to split with an axe or maul. Daddy apparently didn't think much of sycamore as wood or building material either because I can't remember him ever cutting one. Maybe he just thought they were too pretty to put a saw blade into.

The hardwoods and pines that thrived in the hopscotching maneuvers of Daddy's forestry weren't all that random. The sylvan cycle of felling, cutting, loading, splitting, and burning was a year-round thing. The industry was hard work and the genesis of my understanding that in order to have something for later, you'd best make what you have now last. Daddy's selection of trees to cut was an illustration of a land ethic being practiced. Certain hardwoods were most valuable. Red oaks, cut up, split, and dried, made the best firewood. Inhaling the pleasantly rank odor that came from a section of scarlet oak freshly laid open with a sledgehammer and maul was like sniffing smelling salts in the chill fall air. In the wood heater or laid across the fireplace andirons (we called them fire dogs), cured red oak popped and burned hot enough to quickly take the cold edge off a room. White oaks, especially young, straight, tall-growing ones, were reserved for construction. A twelve-foot log split in half lengthwise made sturdy railings for the feedlot corral. Hickories burned well, too, but were much harder to split and so they were cut sparingly. Sometimes Daddy made tool handles out of small ones because they were tough and lasted a long time. He'd save the dried hickory shavings and use them to smoke meat on the grill. Though Daddy cut trees for the services they could render, I'd like to think that he also found some soul-satisfying recognition of their beauty and usefulness as living beings.

If Mamatha's house was the heart of the Home Place, Daddy's hard labor was the breath that made its blood bright. Once the trees were down and chopped up, Jock and I moved in to split and load. Much of what we cut was bound for Mamatha's old cast-iron cookstove. An antiquity even back then, it had probably been state of the art sometime in the early 1880s and stood on four stumpy legs like a black-and-white cow. The tiny kitchen where the stove stood was an orderly mess of culinary clutter. Cast iron skillets sat beside modern aluminum pots and pans. Plastic canisters and bowls covered the counters. Cabinets and a rolltop pantry overflowed with canned goods and bags of dried peas and beans. Enough food had been hoarded to feed us until Jesus came back for his *next* last supper.

There was other stuff in that kitchen that had probably been around for almost a hundred years. A boatlike wooden basin that had belonged to my great-grandmother Big Mama was frequently the focus of Mamatha's kitchen attentions. Like her mother before her, she'd pour flour, buttermilk, and some shortening into it—Big Mama had probably used lard—and work it back and forth with her knotty fingers until a mound of clayey white dough emerged. The dough rolled flat, perforated with the mouth of a jelly glass, and fed into the belly of the stove became hot buttermilk biscuits. Buttered up and slathered in sticky, sweet molasses, there was nothing better. And accompanied by a plate of grits and maybe some fried calf's liver and onions with gravy, the biscuits gave me just cause to spend most Saturday mornings at the Ramshackle before making my way to the Ranch. When I stayed for lunch, there might be fried-bologna sandwiches and potato salad.

Breakfast and lunch were always good. Dinner, though, was on a separate level of delightful gluttony. Mamatha often started cooking it right after breakfast, to take advantage of the already hot stove and to let the flavors meld and marinate for hours. Garden-grown string beans and red-skinned white potatoes, fresh tomato and creamed corn soup, fried crookneck squash and green spring onions, baked macaroni and cheese pie, roast beef, and corn-bread might all make up a single glorious meal. Top that off with a crusty peach cobbler, molasses bread, lemony tea cakes, creamy sweet potato pie, or some ancient but delicious butter-drenched pound cake dug from the lower-room freezer: my waistline quickly expanded into a Sears "Husky" size.

Cooking the way Mamatha did took time and she never rushed food to the table. Convenience and impatience were not excuses for eating poorly. We always ate at the table. Even though Daddy eventually bought my grandmother an electric stove, it sat unused because she didn't trust it to cook the "right" way. To her fast food meant the meal would be ready in an hour—or two. I'm not sure Mamatha ever touched a hamburger or fry that didn't come from a Home Place cow or homegrown potato. If she did I'll bet she thought that it was somehow the devil's doing.

Mamatha never would've cooked so much food for herself alone. The never-ending buffet was her way of keeping me around. It was a simple formula: she cooked, I ate. The bribery mostly worked. The food was fuel for adventures to come. From the kitchen table the woods and fields beckoned.

A chilly October morning is an undeniable temptation to any wild-loving seeker. But a Saturday with ice-frosted fields and storms of colorful leaves swirling about makes the undeniable irresistible. Unchained from school obligations, there were only my chores to struggle through. I tried to fly through the bed making, wood chopping, floor sweeping, and whatever else Mamatha dreamed up, to get outside as quickly as possible. Like cooking and eating, though, housework was not a place for rushing. I can still hear her mantra: "When a job is once begun, never leave it 'til it's done. Be the labor great or small, do it well or not at all."

When the chores were finally done, however, I could break free of the house and enter a fantasy world of earth and sky. The path to those places wound past a big pecan tree, where roving gangs of noisy blue jays conducted morning raids to gather a share of nuts. Pecans were a coveted Home Place commodity, since they yielded sweet holiday pies. The bold jay mobs disrupted that flow and Mamatha took it personally, frequently blasting away at the birds with her .410 shotgun. A few paid for the robberies with their lives but the raids never ended and the pies kept coming, too. There seemed to be enough pecans to go around. Just beyond the pecan tree there was a mucky, smelly feedlot where Daddy fattened up steers for slaughter. Luckily for me, a boy who had more than enough work to keep him occupied, we were spared the squeezing and squirting that milk cows demanded.

Much of the Home Place was fenced. Walking the cow path through the pasture and the creek bottom was a quick way to check the fence line for breaks without interrupting the day's exploration. If I couldn't somehow splice a repair or prop up a leaning post I'd report the broken place to Daddy when I finally got to the Ranch. Before I got too deep into the woods, I might take a few minutes to lie in the pasture lane, enticing the "buzzards" to investigate. I lay as still as I could and did my best imitation of something stinking and dead. Once or twice the ruse worked and I could almost count the feathers in the broad black wings and see the bare red heads twisting to investigate before my nerve shriveled. I miraculously revived to run away before the vultures could peck my eyes out, like Mamatha had warned me they'd do. I felt closer to flight by bringing the birds nearer to my earthbound existence. Watching those scavengers tracing circles in the sky was hypnotic. I often wished we could trade places, that I could sail as effortlessly on the wind as they did.

Teasing vultures and imagining flight, I strolled along pasture paths and through forests and fields. The days seemed endlessly long and way too short at the same time. I'd walk for hours before showing up at the Ranch and no one would ask me where I'd been. Days, weeks, months, seasons, and years on the Home Place passed and every moment offered new lessons. It was a time of freedom and discovery.

On the Home Place there were rolling fields of waist-high

green rye and sun-ripened wheat to run through. I sometimes pretended that the cows in the pasture were a herd of bison on a western prairie. I was a Plains hunter, Lakota, stalking the woolly beasts. And then some days I was "Jim"—Jim Fowler, the young, brave wildlife adventurer on *Mutual of Omaha's Wild Kingdom*. Jim was always being sent into danger by the show's white-haired, whiny-voiced host, Marlin Perkins—wrestling huge anacondas or wrangling rhinos. There were mysterious creeks with hidden creatures lurking underneath the water's surface and endless blue skies with hawks soaring in plain sight. I wanted to see it all.

I can still hear the quail calling and the foxes barking. I can still taste the sweetness of blackberries plucked fresh off the bramble and smell the rain coming on the approaching rumble of a summer-evening storm. All that and the land were *mine* back then. I was the richest boy in the world, a prince living right there in backwoods Edgefield. Two hundred acres. The Lanham family's land was a boyhood barony—our kingdom. It was a place where the *real* wild things dwelled.

The memories run deep. The Home Place was where Cheves Creek snaked foamy and quick and where Daddy taught us to fish. Wetting a line, hoping for a bream to take a wormy hook; calling the cows in from evening pasture; picking butter beans on a sweaty summer's eve, with a trip to the Augusta Exchange Club Fair hanging in the balance; stacking heavy bales of sweet-smelling Bermuda hay; watching a flock of wary wild turkeys grazing the spring growth; busting up the side-hill covey of quail for the hundredth time; dirt-clod wars with Jock and Bug that I never seemed to win; mowing an acre of grass for a dollar; a toddling little sister meandering into the strawberry patch to pick her own sweet treats; the belly-filling satisfaction of homegrown food and thirst-slaking coolness of spring water; the awe of a whitetail leaping the blacktop road in a single bound; the wonder of finding an ancient arrowhead in a newly plowed field; the breathtaking beauty of the bluest jay against golden hickory leaves. All of these Home Place things haunt me pleasantly. They are ghosts I conjure up from time to time to help me understand who I am and perhaps recapture who I need to be.

They say that home is where the heart is. Now with that place far removed in time and space and my present life firmly planted in suburbia and lethargy-inducing convenience, I recall those times and most of what came with them wistfully. My heart has moved on to love other people, places, and things like I never thought I could. But that first place I knew as home will always be locked within.

Mamatha Takes Flight

The supernatural is the natural not yet understood.
— Elbert Hubbard

EVOLUTION. IT'S HOW WE ADAPT TO WHAT THE WORLD throws at us. We've netted physical dividends—bigger brains and opposable thumbs—from years of change. Technology, on the other hand, is how we master the world, but it often masters us in return. We're an aspirational species, never giving up on enhancing the richness and reach of our lives. That effort drives the course of history: revolutions, wars, elections, assassinations, and innovations.

We have come to walk upright and we have discovered fire— or at least how to use it. That is who we are as a species: not just aspirational but at a unique edge between evolution and technology. We adapt, we master; we are part of nature, we overcome it; we are shaped by history, we make it. And any one of our stories can thus be told twice, looking at the forces outside us and those within. So it is with Daddy's mother: my grandmother Mamatha. She was a woman who straddled nine decades and all of the history and social evolution that came along with them. I was a witness to three decades of her life but, through her eyes, was privileged enough to see much more than that.

In my lifelong obsession with flight, I've had occasion to consider both evolution and technology. Through the aeons birds have gained feathers and wings. That most have also become airborne over millions of years is truly miraculous.

Humans, of course, did not evolve to join them. For the relatively short time we've shared the earth with birds, we've looked skyward and wondered about—maybe wished for—flight. But we couldn't solve the mysteries of lift and propulsion. Then, a little over a century ago, we made some of the fastest progressions from dreaming to doing that mankind has ever witnessed. In the span of a few decades, the dreams of taking flight became a reality.

Mamatha was born Ethel Jennings in 1896—one generation removed from slavery. She entered life on the edge between two centuries, in a nation that was expanding rapidly as a world power. Technology had already conquered much of the continent via rail and steam engine. Automobiles were replacing horses and voices were streaming in crackling tones along telephone cables. It must've been a heady time, with all the connectivity broadening horizons in some ways and making the world smaller in others.

For some flying things it was also the worst of times. By the 1890s the same technologies that allowed people to move faster and further and tell others where they'd been and were going led to the extinction of the passenger pigeon. Word of mouth—expedited and expanded by a growing phone system, or a few dots and dashes tapped on a telegraph message—about where the dwindling flocks had congregated made it easy for greedy shooters to slaughter the last of a species that had once darkened the skies. Other endangered birds suffered, too. Carolina parakeets, noisy native parrots that found comfort in big cypress bottoms and around cocklebur-infested farmsteads, were also disappearing. Unabated logging of swamps pushed the green-and-gold masses of sociable birds to the brink. Steam shovels drained the water away and the sawyers did the rest—cutting and bucking and running wood out on rails to build the nation. The parakeets soon had no place to go. In just a few short years humans would take the empty spaces the birds had left behind in the skies.

It's 1903 now, and Ethel is a little girl, amazed and maybe unbelieving when word washes down through church folk and the rumor mill that some crazy white men in North Carolina are flying like birds—but in a machine made of wood and cloth! I'm sure there were those who didn't like it, who saw the sky as a place God made for feathered things, not man. This flying thing was an affront to God—sinful arrogance—and surely would not last. Those people would have been wrong, of course. Godly or not, humankind was off the ground.

Fourteen years later, in 1918, Ethel is hanging the wash out to dry in the warm sun, wondering if her husband-to-be, Joseph Samuel Lanham—"Daddy Joe"—will come home from the war alive. She knows from newspapers—and letters from France—that men with designs on destroying one another are conquering the air with deadly effect. She reads and hopes for the best. An odd puttering sound overhead interrupts Ethel's work and drowns out the copycat song of a mockingbird. A biplane growls and crawls below the clouds. She shades her eyes against the midday sun with tired hands and waves. The unseen pilot waggles the plane's wings in a salute from heaven. Not long afterward, Joseph comes home from France alive, but not whole.

Less than a decade later and flight is no longer a novelty to Ethel or Joseph. Charles Lindbergh flew an airplane across an ocean she's never seen. The world celebrated the achievement but to Ethel it seemed simply another thing done by white men with too much time on their hands. At home there were three girls to raise, a farm to help keep and, in a little more than a year, another mouth—a son's—to feed.

"Time flies" goes the saying, and Ethel is forty-eight and wondering if an even bigger war will ever end. The Nazis claim racial superiority and work hard to rid Europe of anyone not fitting their designs. The Japanese attack Pearl Harbor. Joseph and Ethel hear about black aviators—trained down in Alabama—who are taking the fight to the Germans. Joseph knows of the famous black college in Tuskegee and even follows the farming prescriptions of a professor there named George Washington Carver, who advises plowing on the contour and planting cover crops to save the soil. The black airmen have endured hatred, but are proving themselves in airplanes that can fly faster than any bird ever imagined. They surpass the records of many of their white counterparts. Ethel and Joseph talk frequently about their hopes for better times and imagine that achievements like the soldiers' flying and fighting and the Tuskegee professor's farming genius will help set things right once and for all.

As the demands of war call for more wood, large swaths of bottomland forest disappear for the sake of Uncle Sam. Ivory-billed woodpeckers hold on until the last, but the "Lord God" birds finally disappear as another world war fades into promises of "never again."

Just a few years later, however, Joseph and his wife are sending their drafted only son into conflict. President Truman calls it a "police action" but people are dying by the thousands over a line drawn in the Asian dirt and something called "communism." The parents fret again over a war threatening to destroy something they love.

The only Lanham son skirts by the conflict, though, serving

out a lucky deferment to Europe. After a stint in Germany, he returns to Edgefield to find his father ailing. There's an uneasiness boiling up across the nation, too. A quiet seamstress sits down on a bus in Alabama and a man named Martin Luther King Jr. seems intent on making things happen for colored folk as quickly as the supersonic jets arc across the sky, leaving long trails of white and sound in their wake. A birdwatcher named Rachel Carson writes a book warning that our sins against nature—polluting land, water, and air with chemicals—will create silent springs and disaster for all living things. There's talk in the newspapers about man-made machines circling the earth.

Joseph struggles to see the 1960s come in and doesn't get to share in Dr. King's dreams for equality. The veteran has done his part, though, training his people to lead, learn, and teach their way to better lives. My grandfather dies maybe hearing more saber rattling—of missiles on Cuba that fly faster than any airplane he's ever known. This man, who once crouched in a trench and saw leather-helmeted men in open-air cockpits dogfighting over muddy battlefields in planes that moved barely faster than an automobile, might have mused sadly in his last days over a potential destruction that no one will see or hear coming.

Ethel is almost seven decades removed from the little girl's disbelief that men were flying, and on some days the air over her gray-haired head seems more filled with the sound of airplanes than birdsong. Her husband has been dead eight years but there's another Joseph with her now, a little namesake grandson only four years old. On a humid July night in 1969—only a little more than a year since the shocking death of Dr. King—there's another war going on and young people protesting everywhere, for and against everything. The people seem restless. There's a buzz about white men doing something in the sky again and Mamatha stops reading her Bible to turn on her small television. There in grainy black and white, a man in a strange suit walks on the moon. She ponders what her husband would've thought; she asks what little Joseph thinks. She thanks God, grateful for living to see humanity somehow get closer to the heavens. She wonders aloud in that prayer, asks Jesus for just a little measure of such progress in the lives of a people who still can't find happiness because of the color of their skin.

In her ninety-six years Mamatha was a witness to the extremes of good and bad that humanity visits on itself. She watched war and peace cycle like the seasons. She saw night-riding Klansmen terrorizing to oppress a people and a tired Birmingham seamstress sitting down to help those same people stand up. She believed in the promise of a crucified Messiah who would return to save us all from sin and had faith in a man named King to deliver a different sort of salvation. She buried her only husband and somehow outlived her only son. Maybe it takes a bit of magic to get through almost a century of that kind of life. I can imagine that for all the miracles of flight she lived through, on some days a soaring hawk or a singing thrush was more than enough to measure her life by.

As Mamatha watched flight advance from feathers to fantasy over nearly a century, she remained steadfast in certain beliefs. As amazing as those technologies must have seemed to her, they were something tangible, requiring no faith beyond the witnessing. There were phenomena, though, that she set store in and lived by, which defied science and technology.

To say my grandmother was a witch might be a bit of a stretch. But she was at the very least a conjurer with a foot in two dimensions—this world and the spirit one. Why else would anyone have nightly conversations with the dead, live steeped in superstition, and use an array of concocted potions, herbal remedies, and incantations to treat illness as readily as anyone else would use over-the-counter drugs?

A hat tossed on the bed, dirt swept out the door past dusk, or a careless step over an abandoned broom were high crimes in Mamatha's house. Beyond the bad luck were far worse things. Lying on the floor was forbidden lest someone step over you and stunt your growth. A broom swept across your feet could mean an early death. An owl hooting in the yard or a bird trapped inside the house warned of death to come. A "blood moon" meant end times were approaching. Spilled salt, broken mirrors, and things that went bump in the night were all a part of her daily routine, her dos and don'ts—the supernatural accepted as normal. The superstitions that controlled so much of Mamatha's existence weren't in the least confounded by her staunchly Christian faith. She never confused the two.

When I eventually left the Home Place, I entered the modern world still believing that ill-placed hats and road-crossing black cats could determine whether things went my way.

My grandmother was eighty-four when I left for Clemson University. She died twelve years later, but she had always seemed old to me, with her constant complaints of aches and pains. I can't remember her ever standing fully upright. She ambled along with a shuffling gait, swaying slightly from side to side and stooped over like some spell-spinning witch from a fairy tale. Her joints were stiffened with arthritis. Even though she regularly lubed up her knees, shoulders, and elbows with strong-smelling balms and liniments, she never got anywhere fast. Maybe the difficulties came from working in the fields long ago. Chopping rows of cotton and too many hours bent over a boiling cauldron full of lye soap and dirty clothes had taken their toll.

Mamatha's gently furrowed face reflected a history that spanned most of the twentieth century—all of its jubilation, pain, fear, wars, and "*rumors* of wars," as she liked to say. She had lived through them all.

When Daddy Joe was drafted, he served in the American Expeditionary Forces "over there," with one of the few black American units to see combat in that war. Although black men have served heroically in every American conflict since the Revolution, there always seems to be something more to prove. Daddy Joe was up to the task and true to the heroes' legacy, somehow surviving the terrors of trench warfare; going "over the top" into machine gun fire, artillery barrages, and gas attacks; and living daily in fear and filth with rats, disease, and the threat of horrific wounding or death. When the 371st Regiment, Company C, went to Europe, the US Army assigned them to the French; blacks, they thought, didn't have the mettle to fight alongside white Americans. But the 371st distinguished themselves in combat, killing, capturing, and conquering Germans in some of the most vicious battles of the war. In the Verdun they earned a unit award of the Croix de Guerre with Palm. The unit won not only medals but respect as men from their French commanders.

Daddy Joe came home with wounds to his body, scars in his memory—and a newfound respect for life, motivating a legacy of more peaceful pursuits. Mamatha married Daddy Joe in 1919, not long after he returned to a nation where black men were harassed and hanged for simply wearing their uniforms in public. And so Daddy Joe left the war behind and turned his attention to family and farming.

I'm sure Ethel saw her new husband's pain, listened to his stories of the horrors of war, and maybe assured him—and herself—that times would get better. Mamatha often told me stories about Daddy Joe and the war, pulling out old photo albums and letters. There were other artifacts of his service around, too—the eerie gas mask, and a rusting soup-bowl-like helmet that had sheltered him from shot and shrapnel. But I was always most struck by a couple of colorized photographs of a proud, dark-skinned man in a dough-boy uniform. He was lean and fit in his olive-green woolen jacket and pants, his overseas cap cocked to the side and the leggings they called puttees wrapped neatly like bandages up to his knees. Handsomely bookish in round, wire-rimmed glasses, Daddy Joe probably posed for the photo before the realities of life in combat took hold. I marveled at the courage it must have taken—to simply be a black man in Edgefield at a time when its political leaders were sanctioning terror for "negroes" who dared step outside the lines, and then to dutifully fight for a home country that despised him for his black skin. It was brave, beyond brave, heroic.

Daddy Joe used to wax on and on to Mamatha about his time in Paris, where his color was celebrated and rights weren't restricted by race. It must've been a heady thing for a black man to walk those streets with no one paying attention to him, no one calling him *nigger* or *boy*. Mamatha said he'd even tried to convince her that they should move back there. I often wondered what would have become of me, of us, of the Home Place had Daddy Joe decided to become "Monsieur Joseph"—a man not limited by color or by America's dim view of it. In the end, though, there was the pull of kin and familiarity. Maybe there was also something he missed about working the soil and watching things grow. He was better suited to nurturing life.

Mamatha was a gifted worrier and probably fretted over Daddy Joe's fragile health. There were also stresses at home, children, crops, and cattle to tend to. Daddy Joe and Mamatha bore three children, a trio of girls: Louise, Pearl, and Ruby. Near the end of their first decade together, in the autumn of 1928, they welcomed their fourth child and only son, James Hoover. The little boy was a particular treasure, the sole hope that the Lanham name would continue. Almost exactly one year later, the Great Depression followed Hoover into the world.

Daddy Joe went on to teach and farm. He plowed and planted; herded, harrowed, and harvested. He became the principal of a school and trained a "who's who" of the future leaders of the black community in Edgefield. He was respected by everyone and stood tall as a dependable man who did his best by his family, community, and country. I wish I'd had the honor of meeting him, but he died before I was born.

Most of what I know about Daddy Joe came through Mamatha's stories of the flesh-and-bone man she called her husband for forty-two years. But I also came to know him in another way. His ghost roamed the Home Place. My grandmother communed with him—and other dead people—on an almost nightly basis, mostly on the quiet edges of the day, in the "witching" hours when things are still. Sometimes Daddy Joe tried to reclaim his place in their wedding bed, she said, stretching out beside her "icy cold as steel." At other times a subtle shadow passing through the moonlight, or something mysteriously falling in another room, alerted her to ghostly wanderings. Whatever forms the visitations took, they were was scary as hell and I spent nights buried under a protective fortress of covers with only my mouth and nose exposed as breathing snorkels. Even in the sweat-wrenching swelter of a midsummer's night, with nothing to cool the room except a window fan, I'd burrow under layers of bed linens thinking that they'd somehow keep the haints at bay.

One night, as Mamatha began one of her conversations, I finally mustered the nerve to poke my head from underneath the quilts. Sure enough, there was something standing in the bedroom doorway. Faceless and backlit by the tiny night-light in the next room, it stretched its arms across the doorway as if to brace itself between two dimensions. I opened my eyes wide to make sure it wasn't a dream. Mamatha confirmed my fears when she addressed the thing by name: "Joseph? Joseph? What you want, Joseph?" I watched and listened, terrified, until it vanished into the darkness.

Mamatha talked about the visit matter-of-factly over biscuits and bacon the next morning, like she always did—the meetings were completely ordinary for her. I wonder now how much of the activity she solicited. There weren't any Ouija boards or special incantations I ever heard, but I'm not sure Mamatha ever denied the visitors passage into her world, either. For years stories of ghosts and spirits were simply a part of nightly routines and family gatherings. Almost everyone had seen, heard, or felt something. Ghost horses and mystical mules galloped invisibly around houses. Children saw death angels and died soon after. The appearance of glowing green orbs and encounters with things that bumped and thumped in the night were expected. Even Daddy, typically a stoic tower of reason and rationality, told stories of inexplicable phenomena that gave me second thoughts about walking around anywhere on the Home Place after dark.

Daybreak was a welcome relief from the spooky socializing. Not that the magic stopped with the light of day—it simply changed form to something less frightening. Mamatha, like many other older people, depended on an assortment of drugs to quell various ailments. She took a familiar cocktail of pills, to keep her high blood pressure in check, her heart rhythm regular, and her back from aching. But Mamatha supplemented the standard stuff with remedies no store sold. She preferred out of the ground to over the counter.

A bounty of innocuous-looking plants grew right outside the back door and provided free and often effective alternatives to what the doctors prescribed. Things most would call weeds—mullein with its soft, wooly leaves; pokeweed, which grew head high and had purple berries; and feathery-looking dog fennel—all of it had a higher purpose in Mamatha's world. Mullein tea and pokeweed, properly prepared, were both general tonics for whatever ailed a body. The pungent green plumes of the fennel, crushed and rubbed on insect stings, eased pain and swelling quickly. Mamatha removed unsightly moles by tying them off with cow's-tail hair tourniquets and quieted coughs with a warm shot of whiskey and honey. A teaspoon of sugar did help the medicine go down—but even when sugar preceded a dose of turpentine to clear congestion, there was little to feel delighted about. I was often plagued with painful tongue ulcers that Mamatha diagnosed as lie bumps. She prescribed truth as the best cure, but beyond that she would either painfully snatch them off with her fingernails or paint my tongue with nasty-tasting tinctures that hurt as much as the malady itself. She boiled roots to make salves for my fungal infections and believed that ardent prayer could heal anything.

Being a growing, feral boy, my demand for calories was constant.

What with all the running, jumping, climbing, exploring, wood chopping, hay stacking, and fence mending that might fill a single day, I needed as much fuel as I could get. I never met a cookie, pie, cake, candy bar, or slab of gravy-covered meat I wouldn't eat. In truth I was a greedy kid, putting away as much as Mamatha would feed me and then scarfing down more for good measure.

But a half dozen butter-soaked biscuits swimming in molasses, accompanied by enough bacon, grits, and cheesy scrambled eggs to feed three people, can cause problems. Sometimes things bubbled and boiled inside me and became painful beyond what my physiology or anything from a bottle might cure.

Mamatha's solution wasn't pink and couldn't be delivered by the teaspoon. Instead she turned to a different prescription—one filled from somewhere "out there." The treatment began with a series of circles drawn on my bare belly, spiraling outward from my navel. With the abdominal art completed, Mamatha started tracing lines in the air to make two or three imaginary crosses. As my paunch rumbled she muttered words that I never understood. After the incantations, she drew an invisible string gently upward from my belly button, until the pain was gone. That magic never failed.

When I'm in an old field full of things most others simply bypass as weeds, I see healing. I can't help grabbing a piece of dog fennel just to smell its pungent perfume. A mess of poke salad is better than any pot of gourmet greens, and a piece of cornbread alongside brings back vivid memories of times with Mamatha. I tell whoever will listen of the curative qualities of the botanical apothecary that grows all around us. Some relatives used to say that Mamatha's cures and incantations came from ancestors who brought healing traditions from the Motherland or learned them as slaves. Other relatives claimed they were born of some American

Indian connection. I call it a mystery: I'm not sure where her magic came from and probably never will be.

I grew up understanding that the mysterious things I experienced didn't all need to be explained. Not knowing everything was OK. But since I last fell under any of my grandmother's spells, I've been trained extensively. Some might even say I've been overtrained, brainwashed to think critically about the natural world. As a scientist, I was taught that the unexplained is to be pursued relentlessly and hell-bent on publishing. My training suggests that if mysteries can't be unraveled, then perhaps what we see isn't "real"; if the results aren't publishable, then the observed isn't believable.

Mamatha's alchemy wouldn't have passed the muster of peer review—but she wouldn't have cared. In the midst of amazing advancements that saw flight evolve from fantasy to commonplace, she believed unshakably that some things existed beyond explanation. But her magic wasn't just about the metaphysical. It was most evident in her ability to turn bad to good, to see life through death and hope through despair—and to see the Home Place through history, becoming a refuge for my family.

A Good Name

A good name is rather to be chosen than great riches,
and loving favor rather than silver and gold.

⟞ Proverbs 22:1

In 1928, THE YEAR MY FATHER WAS BORN, HERBERT HOOVER
completed his tenure as Secretary of Commerce and was
elected president. J. Edgar Hoover was director of the Bureau of
Investigation, which he would help turn into the FBI seven years
later. It was a good time to bestow the name "Hoover" on a son for
whom you had great hopes. But when the reckless abandon of the
Roaring Twenties came to a screeching halt, "Hoover" rapidly lost
its currency as a name. The presidential Hoover, Herbert, was the
man in charge as the nation sunk eyeball deep into the most mis-
erable years of the Depression. The law-enforcing Hoover, J. Edgar,
used and abused the law to the furthest extent of his eccentric will
for almost fifty years. These were poor namesakes; "Hoover" was
not an auspicious star under which to begin.

James Hoover Lanham, however, was my father. There were
other names people called him: "James," "James H.," "Trap," "Ish,"
"Big Chief," "Daddy." According to Mamatha her Hoover was something of a prodigy, sitting in his father's classroom at Bettis Academy
among much older children. Hoover must've been a sponge, soaking
up everything he could from schoolbooks and at Daddy Joe's side. He
read, ciphered, and studied his way into joining the best, brightest,
and boldest that black Edgefield had to offer.

The Lanham boy probably wasn't ever a hell-raiser. In all likelihood he was obedient to a father-loving fault. In the Lanham family dutifulness is a valued commodity. It can be traded for all sorts of highly sought-after things otherwise difficult to gain: praise, freedom, and favor. Daddy Joe and Mamatha heaped a shit-ton of all three on their only son. He could do no wrong; he was dependable, respectful, intelligent, and strong. He was the golden boy cast in burnished bronze. Even his three older sisters—Louise, Pearl, and Ruby—looked up to the child some would later claim was born grown.

Hoover was a child during the Great Depression and came of age at the height of World War II. What was it like growing up in a world where despair was the common cry for almost two decades? When the prairie soils blew east on dust bowl winds, how did Mamatha and Daddy Joe convince their children that there was hope beyond the clouds of dirt falling from the sky? I wonder what the thirteen-year-old Hoover thought about as news of the attack on Pearl Harbor arrived. Did word of the battles raging across the globe frighten him? Did stories of a maniac talking of a white super-race make him fearful for his black future? Did he know where places like Berlin, Paris, Guadalcanal, or Okinawa were before young men went there to kill or be killed? What was daily life like as shortages, rationing, and other widening ripples of the war hit home? Was Hoover inspired when he heard about black men being given the chance to fight with guns, as soldiers, rather than with pots and brooms, as cooks and cleaners? Did it seem like the world was going to end when a bomb might destroy cities in a single flash? Did his father ever talk to Hoover about the horrors of battle and how the war he'd fought in was supposed to end all other wars—but didn't?

Hoover grew up in a world of turmoil. As the radio spilled Duke Ellington's and Count Basie's big band tunes rumor must've spun horrific stories of all the inhumane things happening in far-away places. As the war finally ended and Hoover was nearing manhood at seventeen, maybe there was a hope growing that the world hadn't experienced in almost twenty years. After Bettis, an optimistic Hoover headed to Claflin College in Orangeburg, South Carolina, to get a college degree and make his own way forward.

But then another war broke out. The threat of a former ally's communist ideology, a "red scare," led to the Korean Conflict. Hoover was done with college and had to go. But a technicality took him away from the battle lines, as I've mentioned, and sent him to Europe instead.

There are a few pictures of Hoover in Germany. Relieved of the horrors his father had seen in the trenches of France, but also of the responsibilities of farm and Home Place, he was released to become the man his buddies called "Ish." I love the photos that show him smiling in the middle of some good time. In one he's on ski patrol, a black man in the white snow. The wide grin on his face matches the powder he's posed against, looking ready to take off on some mission. It looks more like fun than duty to me. Another picture shows him locked in a card game. There's a cigarette hanging onto a half-cocked smile that gives away what must've been a nice hand and an even better time. I can almost hear "Ish" chuckling at the prospect of the win and maybe some bet.

Where did all of that free-flowing laughter go? I suppose the responsibilities waiting for Ish back home, once the pretty frau-leins disappeared and farming and family became the priority, took some of that away. Life turned a corner. An ailing father and an increasingly dependent mother meant he was Hoover again.

Back in Edgefield Hoover exerted himself to extremes to ensure that the Home Place was taken care of. In the midst of all the work: Rosa Parks. Martin Luther King Jr. A president is assassinated. Then his brother is gunned down. King is killed and Malcolm X, tuned into change, loses his life for the cause, too. Slithering in and around all of this is a war in a small country called Vietnam. People march and protest. The world must seem in utter turmoil again— but Hoover nurtures the Home Place, begins a career, takes a wife, begins to make a family, and marches for dignity, too. He's making a name that anyone who meets him won't ever forget.

I think about all of this when I imagine who James Hoover Lanham was—and who he became. To me Hoover was everyman: teacher, coach, mechanic, plumber, cattleman, farmer, lumberjack, husband, brother, son, and father. He had to be all those things because his family's survival depended on the plowing, cutting, feeding, loading, and fixing that made things go and grow.

"Hoover" comes from the German word *Huber*, and means landowner or prosperous small farmer. In this my father fulfilled his name in ways Herbert and J. Edgar did not. The Home Place was James Hoover's country. The forests, fields, and creeks were his providences to protect. Crop failures and bottomland floods were no less a challenge when scaled down to two hundred acres than national crises of dust bowls and Mississippi River floods were to any president. My father's courage and leadership in the efforts to fence things up or make straight furrows meant everything for us. He seldom failed.

Hoover became my Daddy in January 1965. From the earliest times that I can remember he was someone I wanted to emulate and please. Mamatha constantly stressed the importance of not disappointing Hoover. And so as soon as I was able I became a sticky shadow, following him when he would allow it, wishing I could go with when he wouldn't. When he worked, I watched. Where he asked, I assisted. On cold nights when the pipes froze and the water stopped flowing, I'd tote the tools or hold the flashlight while Daddy dug through the mud to find the leak that drained the pressure. I stood watching in bone-shivering awe as he worked through the discomfort of wet and cold without complaint. Now and then I'd sneak peeks beyond the beam of the flashlight for monsters hiding in the dark. The Big Chief didn't fear the scary things that lurked in the night; I thought maybe they were afraid of him.

I saw my father as some sort of superhuman being. Hoover was a giant, tossing heavy bales of hay like toy blocks and wrestling bawling calves to the ground like running backs. In the woods he was a burly brown Paul Bunyan wielding growling chain saws, sharp axes, and heavy mauls like they were extensions of his own arms. He'd cut and saw and chop, yelling "Timberrrrrrrr!" as mighty oaks crashed to the ground. Nothing was ever minimal effort. He'd sweat through his clothes in deepest February like it was mid-August. In warm weather the water would run off his brow in salty streams as he shredded the earth into ribbons behind his John Deere tractor. He sat astride that snorting green metal beast as if it were a monstrous draft horse, urging it on with throttle and reining it in with clutch and brake. Sometimes, when the plow mired in the stubborn clay, the tricycle-wheeled steed would protest and rear up dangerously on its big hind tires. Hoover would sit in the saddle, calm and in total control of an unruly machine that was a notorious farmer killer. No one else could handle the tractor like he did. Hardly anyone else was ever allowed to try. The only time I got to ride was when I was a little boy, and he'd hoist me up to sit in his lap to steer. It was rare close contact.

I marveled at each and every feat of derring-do. Inclement weather was simply another obstacle to overcome. He tamed that wild place just enough to make life safe and comfortable. Something useful could always be manufactured out of the useless. In the moments when things were getting fixed or fed, repaired or ripped apart, plowed or pushed down, he was an unstoppable force who seemed to bend the world to his bidding.

There was more to Hoover than the physical, though. He threw arcane quotes around like chunks of wood. He'd picked up lines from the epic poem *Beowulf* and knew enough German to sound like he'd made good time of his years in the military. The guttural tongue came naturally to him and I'd imitate it at school to impress ten-year-olds who didn't know any better. An "auf Wiedersehen" dropped here or "guten Tag" sprinkled there made me sound worldly. Being an Edgefield country boy in sophisticated suburban Aiken, I needed all the help I could get.

Geology was a hobby of Hoover's, too. You were as likely to hear "igneous," "rift," and "inclusion" at the Ranch as anything else. All around the house were rocks from near and far. He was constantly gathering specimens: quartz, feldspar, mica, and other things with odd names. He would happily explain how the little treasure came to be millions of years ago and how it had settled where it was now. A collection of arrowheads and other American Indian artifacts that he'd collected would've been fawned over by any museum. There was even a bit of the intrepid explorer in Hoover. From time to time he pulled out a mysterious little black sack that was supposed to hold a precious jewel mined on one of his expeditions. I think we all secretly believed it would be cashed in one day to make us rich, kind of like the Beverly Hillbillies—but black.

Hoover brought back expensive cameras from Germany that

he used religiously even though much more modern gear was available. He fancied himself a photographer in the know and insisted that the old ways were better. I used to sneak into my parents' bedroom closet to check out the thick photography albums he collected as "references." They were filled with artsy pictures of landscapes, celebrities, animals—and naked women. Our house was stacked with books and magazines that covered just about every scientific subject and current events issue. *National Geographic*, *Scientific American*, *Time*, *Life*, and *Newsweek* flowed through the mailbox and the newspaper arrived daily. We had a full set of Compton's Encyclopedias (which I read from *A* to *Z*) and a selection of literary classics to round out the Lanham library. Not learning in that environment would have been hard. Information seeped into your brain without much effort and Hoover, in his never-sated quest to know something about everything, was the one responsible for much of it.

The education went beyond the formal, too. On our fence-mending, water-line-repairing, wood-cutting adventures Hoover would point out this thing or that. There were also science "experiments" in the field, when Hoover decided on-the-go education was worth a break from work. Once, after coming across a timber rattler at the edge of a field he was plowing, he returned to the house to retrieve both us kids and a balloon. He inflated the balloon, tied it to the end of a cane fishing pole, and proceeded to aggravate the coiled snake until it struck and popped the swollen rubber orb. None of us saw the snake move. One moment the serpent was piled up, pissed off, and rattling. The balloon was there—and then suddenly not. It was a magical teaching moment, and the lesson to give rattlers—and the places they liked to hang out—careful and cautious attention stuck fast.

I learned essential woodcraft and field etiquette, too. Important skills like calling cows, splitting ripe oak with an axe, and attention-getting wolf whistling were passed down by example.

My father's J. Edgar Hoover side simmered just beneath his mostly calm and confident exterior. At a hefty six feet two, Hoover was an imposing presence. His stature, booming voice, and take-no-shit attitude were necessary to deal with the seventh and eighth graders he taught daily in his earth sciences classes. For an unruly herd of hormonally confused kids a certain intensity is required. The sharpened edge of his attitude was also probably essential given the resentful peers and constant bouts of bias he faced as one of the few black men teaching in Aiken County, with a level of education that surpassed that of many of the white people he called peers.

Sometimes the intensity followed Daddy home. When it did it could turn into a darker, deep-brooding emotion that could boil over into insult-filled "fussing"—never cussing—or worse. Whoever dared step over Hoover's firmly established line was quickly renamed: a "fool," a "bastard," or someone who "didn't have the sense they were born with." It didn't matter who the offender was. It could be an unruly student tossing spitballs or a dawdling driver improperly signaling a turn. It could be an uncooperative cow that refused to be corralled or it could be one of us kids doing something childish like spilling a drink or breaking a glass. Almost always there was a "Grief!" (no "good" came with it). Sometimes the grumbling was done at a tolerable level in a venting "conversation" with Mama. She sat quietly and let it wind down. But if the line was crossed egregiously enough, the declarations were made at a roaring bull's volume, which would shake your nerves to the root.

The Home Place wasn't a democracy. No one elected James Hoover Lanham to his post. He was born to it. Hoover could be an absolute dictator, whose boundaries were hard-set in concrete. For all his Herculean heroism, for all the knowledge accrued, used, and dispersed by Hoover to others and his family, sometimes the emotional and the physical came together in forceful and unpleasant ways. When fussing failed, there might be a whippin'. There were no time-outs or meaningful conversations to clear up misunderstandings or amend mistakes. Instead, a switch or thick leather belt was often the adjudicator. Most whippin's came from breaking one of three basic rules: obedience, respect, or performance. These were the unmalleable expectations, commandments, that couldn't be bent. Obey all adults. Period. Be respectful to them. Period. Perform tasks at home and work at school to the utmost of your ability. Period.

Obedience was to be given without question to any adult or authority figure. Your job as a child was to be seen and not heard. Respect was to be reflected in classroom conduct that couldn't fall below excellence. Any grade below a B was grounds for a whippin'. A lack of respect was also intelled through a network of relatives, friends, and professional peers who were everywhere and always watching, like an army of spies. A negative report passed to Mama or Daddy was usually met with very little questioning and swift switch action.

Fortunately, the whippin's were few and far between for me. Daddy's heavy voice, hardened with anger and disappointment, was usually enough to put down any thoughts of misbehavior.

I loved my parents, but I've long found it ironic that any black people, coming through the civil rights movement, witnessing all the violence the period brought to bear, and with their parents born at the edge of slavery, would carry the whip forward as a means of control. I've tried to do better with my own children.

I'd like to think Hoover was mostly happy as our Daddy.

Sometimes you could hear it. His laughter was a bass drum rolling. It beat hardest when a bream took the bobber under or the dogs herded the cows without command. Sometimes you could see it. His bright, crooked smile was a full moon shining. The way that I tried to make the drum roll and the moon shine was to have Hoover's good name mirrored in whatever I did. For others to say "That's Hoover Lanham's son" was praise worth more than almost anything to me. In his last few years, though, the laughs were too few and too far between. Maybe, when all's said and done, none of us ever laughs enough.

I worshipped my father but James Hoover Lanham wasn't perfect. There was so much passion for so many things all wound up in a very human wrapping. Complexity inhibits perfection and often destroys it. My father had made mistakes that weighed heavily on him. I believe they drew down the well of happiness that once brimmed to full. Living can drain us. And it always leaves scars. We all incur them. Sometimes we cause them. Daddy created some wounds but did more to heal than hurt.

One night when I was thirteen or fourteen, Daddy was working late to repair the brakes on our 1965 Ford Fairlane. There's always an infinite supply of work to do on a farm and a finite measure of money with which to do it. Sometimes the cars had to go to a mechanic to get repaired but usually not before Hoover did his best to find a lower-cost solution. Daddy lay on the cold ground underneath the car, disassembled auto parts splayed around him. I stood there holding a work lamp, ready to hand him whatever tool he asked for. It was like assisting a surgeon. He'd say "9/16-inch open end" and I'd rummage through the junky toolbox. It made me feel useful and good to help.

Daddy worked hard but that night it seemed like nothing was

going right. Things didn't fit like they were supposed to and time after time something that he had put together had to be taken apart or readjusted. I could feel his frustration growing and knew there were other things weighing on him that he'd never speak of. I'd overheard conversations he and Mama had had about our family. What I didn't know was that worries at work were pulling at him, too. In the shadows and coolness of the evening, where it seemed nearly impossible to me that anyone would be able to put back together what lay apart around us, I wanted to help with more than the proper tool. I wanted desperately to tell Daddy not to worry, that everything would be okay. I wanted to tell him that I wouldn't let him down. I wanted to tell him that I loved him. But I didn't—I never did. We worked on in silence, like always, saying only what was necessary to get the next thing done. There was just the metallic clinking of the tools and what I wished I'd had the courage to say hanging somewhere in the night.

Good and bad, I measure much of who I am by who Hoover was. Mention the name Hoover Lanham around Edgefield and you'll get a response—folks still revere it. They'll reveal or repeat some impressive story of times on the playing field or in the classroom. I suppose that's what Mamatha had envisioned when Hoover was born. She would often tell me that a good name was a priceless thing—worth more than gold. Joseph and Ethel gave their son a name quickly tarnished by others, but my Daddy made it good again.

With the infusion of magic from Mamatha and forging of my own iron will in imitation of Daddy's, I was torqued to be unbalanced, a mystical Type A. Astrologically, an oil-and-water amalgam whose soul is pulled to opposite poles.

What might bring balance to such an unwieldy combination? Grace and an appreciation for the understated are ingredients that can smooth roughness. As Mamatha was showing me that there was more to the world than could be seen and Daddy was hammering the ideal of invincibility deep into my psyche, I learned the art of grace from Mama. Willie Mae Lanham—'Weilk' or 'Jones' (her maiden name) to those who really know her—managed to move mountains when most were still trying to climb them. Beyond might, she possessed a subtle power that enabled her to exist effortlessly in different worlds.

Willie May is the strong and silent type, though she never darkened a doorway with her stature or intimidated a soul with her stare. Instead she's always possessed a quiet fortitude that breaks barriers and silences the naysayers. More than a helpmate, she stood shoulder to shoulder with Daddy. She couldn't measure up to him physically, but she was an equal partner, pulling her weight and more in determining how things went on the Home Place.

A contradiction wrapped in conviction, Mama broke conventions and simultaneously kept tried-and-true traditions alive. In the rural South, a mostly less-than-progressive world where expectations of black women were often focused on home and hearth, she managed expectations by exceeding them. And in the tumultuous 1960s and 1970s—when women began to claim self-esteem, careers, and equality—Mama was fully invested in the liberation movement, gathering graduate degrees and earning professional respect. But there were no undergarments burned or protests joined; Mama never roared. Her stealth feminism was camouflaged by home-sewn clothes and handmade blackberry cobbler.

Willie May's parents, James Milton Jones and Julia Childs Jones, had three children. Willie May sat in between her older sister, Mozelle, and younger brother, Johnnie Arthur. She was a daddy's girl, attentive to the soft-spoken father who began farming his own home place in Ninety Six, South Carolina, after working for the railroad. By all accounts her mother was a funny, straightforward woman who was also ahead of her time in a demure way. They were, according to Willie May, a loving couple. She never heard them argue openly. Her father called his wife "Sis Julia" and she called him "Brer Jim."

Willie May's time on the Ninety Six Home Place was typical of the period. Her parents were raising children in the Depression- and World War II–era South with discipline and education as their priorities, just like Hoover's parents. But important differences in the nature and nurture of Willie May and Hoover made two very different people. She grew up with more options and little of the pressure that Hoover did. The only son of a farm family bears a heavy burden, of carrying on a name and caring for the land. Having a brother who could shoulder such responsibility released Willie May and Mozelle to achieve in ways that many young men could not.

In the late 1940s Willie May left home for Talladega College, an all-black institution founded by former slaves in the foothills of the Alabama Appalachians. It was a bold move for the popular but self-describedly shy homecoming queen to head deeper into the stronghold of segregation. But although the fire of hatred seems always to have burned hotter in Alabama, there have been islands of enlightenment there for black folks. The "Heart of Dixie" is also the home of Booker T. Washington's Tuskegee Institute, now Tuskegee University, where the pioneering conservationist George Washington Carver worked to save the South's soil and black fighter pilots trained to defeat the Third Reich. Talladega is a tiny liberal arts college, nestled north of "Skegee." By the time Willie May got to "Dega," it was an exclusive (and expensive) place—an upper-echelon, ebony-filled ivory tower that prided itself on pushing its students to excellence.

Although she's often described herself as understated, Willie May brags about being a Talladegan. Still, she says she originally stayed away from South Carolina State University, in Orangeburg, because she didn't want to track along behind Mozelle. She wanted to carve her own path. Be different.

Way down in those forested foothills Talladega students were constantly reminded of their obligation to excel and escape the binding conditions of the day. Famed black artist Hale Aspacio Woodruff's murals commemorating the *Amistad* slave mutiny of 1839 and the evolution to justice and freedom are prominently displayed on campus, a source of pride. Perhaps the story of Cinqué and his Mende tribesmen taking control of their own destiny inspired the Talladegans to a greater end. Though the odds were stacked against people of color achieving without extraordinary efforts, Willie May and many of her classmates succeeded. She and her peers became teachers, physicians, professors, attorneys, and civil rights leaders. Armed with degrees from Talladega and then Fisk University in Nashville, Willie May was well equipped with education from two of the most prestigious black colleges in the world. She had to have been brimming with confidence when she came back to South Carolina.

The time spent learning paid off quickly. Willie May was versatile enough to teach math and biology in her first stint in the classroom and was instantly respected for her dedication to the craft. She made friends and influenced people easily in her new job at

W. E. Parker, the colored high school in Edgefield. One of the peers in whom she inspired more-than-professional admiration was a cocky young football coach who'd also just returned home, from an easy Army stint in Germany.

Hoover was good at what he did, too, pushing his athletes to excel beyond the playing field. He was the homegrown boy made hero, returned to make Edgefield better for those coming behind him. But Mama was not impressed. She claims she went about her work quietly and efficiently while Hoover brashly forced his own drive to excel on all who stepped into his shadow. She disliked his arrogant attitude and didn't care much for his looks either. So when there were rumors of Hoover's interest Willie May ignored them. At some point, though, something clicked: a sly glance, a flirtatious word in passing, some mysterious chemistry. A few years later, the professional, platonic relationship had become a marriage, with the first of four children born to continue the Home Place legacy. Willie May's influence made itself felt when she and Hoover traveled west to the University of Oregon to work on graduate degrees. She's always been the quiet encourager, working without fanfare to make life better for everyone.

My mother, with her feet planted firmly in the very different worlds of award-winning biology teacher and of farmwife and homemaker, was like a schizoid superhero—Clark Kent's little-known sister, Clarissa, and her cape-wearing alter ego, Superwoman—equally adept at the finer points of fetal pig dissection and at canning peaches, pears, and peas. The transformation occurred seamlessly and several times on a daily basis. Every morning she got up before everyone else and cooked breakfast. She ironed everyone's clothes; made sure all of us were buttoned, zipped, combed, and coiffed; and did countless other tasks while managing to get herself primly prepped. Once in the car there was no time to waste. The half hour it took to get to school meant checking homework and doling out lunch money between marking up her own students' papers, filling out grade books, and putting the finishing touches on her hair and makeup. By the time Daddy dropped her off at Schofield High the change was complete. She was no longer Mama but Mrs. Lanham. Day after day the transformation occurred, without any acknowledgment from us of the miraculous feats happening before our very eyes.

Together Willie May and Hoover made a unique black American power couple for their time. They were highly educated, highly motivated, and highly respected. Mama seldom wielded the forceful stick of anger or intimidation as Hoover did. Students would say that Mrs. Lanham never raised her voice in the classroom. Instead she gained respect in her own quiet way, a graceful, even-toned and even-tempered glide to excellence and acclaim.

At the end of a long day of herding teenagers there was no rest for the weary. Dinner was always on the table within a couple of hours of getting home. Mama uncomplainingly made her way to the crop fields or garden, picking beans or hoeing weeds with Daddy. Shoulder to shoulder, to make the Home Place life better.

⁓

Mama and Daddy—Willie May Jones and James Hoover Lanham—grew up a fast-flapping crow's half-day flight from one another. From different backgrounds and paths my parents came together to make a family and a world of their own.

Imagine a Norman Rockwell painting. A family gathered around the dinner table—all smiles and good thoughts sealed into the image. Ideals can exist in a painting, where no one moves, breathes, loves, hurts, or hates. The neatly mitered frame encloses reality and keeps its prisoners safe, but also limits what we can see around the edges. From the outside our Home Place family was as close to a black American ideal as it could get: middle class, achieving, and striving to stay together. Around the edges there were imperfections, though. Underneath the pretty layers were mistakes and regrets, painted over.

Stand back. See the imperfect picture for what it is: a work of modern art, created by two artists working with different brushes and different media. We were watercolors bleeding, oils spread, pencil sketched and pen etched. Our lives were painted on a canvas of Home Place forest and field. And in the picture's corner, the signatures—two good names.

A Field Guide to the Four

From childhood, I've relied on field guides to help me appreciate both the stunning and the subtle differences among birds. Even now, I pore over every field guide I can get my hands on—in awe of the diverse catalog of color and form lavishly depicting beings I admire.

Some species' brightly colored feathers allow a birdwatcher to make a call instantly. The first painted bunting I ever saw looked like a palette of spilled oil paints come to life. Posed on a railroad crossing, likely feeding on waste grain, the bird was unmistakable. My hours with the field guide paid off in a sure ID. But then, too, there are look-alikes and closely related species that require more thoughtful inspection. Some songbirds—fall warblers and the drably colored "empid" flycatchers, for example—are notoriously hard to tell apart in the field. Paying attention to the finest details—maybe including a song, chip note, or quirky behavioral clue—is required to parse them.

I belong to *Homo sapiens sapiens*. More particularly, though, I share name and gene with three other members of a special flock: James Jock, Julia Ethelle, and Jennifer Mai. The casual observer might lump us all together under *Homeplace lanhamius* but look closer, as with those warblers, and you'll see we're not always birds of a feather.

As a naturalist, I'm driven to understand the differences between living creatures. So I've occasionally turned to the nearest thing to a field guide of the mind—pop psychology—to understand my siblings. Psychologists label the firstborn as the geniuses—intelligent and ambitious leaders who fly the point of the *v*-shaped flock. They say the youngest siblings are the socialites, seeking attention from others throughout their lives. Those hatched in the middle are the skulkers—low-key introverts bent on pleasing others.

Do these marks fit? You decide. Here is my field guide to the Lanham four.

~

Jock

My brother, Jock, is a genius—a raven whose intelligence and wit chart a different and meandering course through life. Growing up, Jock lived on the edge: building and then deconstructing things only to reassemble them in different ways, or combining chemicals in dangerous, explosive proportions. He listened to Pink Floyd and Ravi Shankar, turning the volume way up so that everyone else in the house listened, too—whether they wanted to or not. He discovered that good mushrooms grew on cow patties and that the Home Place soil could yield more than good beans.

He owned a collection of literature that piqued my curiosity. Carlos Castaneda, Carl Sagan, Kurt Vonnegut, Hugh Hefner, and Larry Flynt sat side by side, offering wisdom and wanton lust. One day when Jock was safely absent from our (theoretically) shared room and the probability of a pummeling reduced to near zero, I went on a mission to find the glossy issues of *Playboy* and *Penthouse* that he secreted away with his Newport menthols. The provocative, full-color photos of naked women occasionally added a thrilling dimension to my twelve-year-old life.

But on that day I didn't get to Miss October. There was a new book on Jock's desk. Unlike the artsy, psychedelic covers that graced most of his novels, the jacket of this book was hardly color-ful. Instead three honking Canada geese were beautifully but sim-ply drawn in blue-green tones. The title was an odd one: *A Sand County* something or other. I flipped through the book and found the most exquisite black-and-white drawings of wild animals. Something about the book snared me, held me in a momentary place that I wanted to be. I didn't read any of the text just then, because time for the mission was growing short. I never, ever wanted to get caught in there; even though the room was supposed to be shared, I still spent most of my time at the Ramshackle and Jock guarded the room as his own. The penalties for being caught would've been serious and painful. But the book was fixed in my mind. And so a few months later, after Jock moved to Boston for college and left the book behind, I took it as my own.

When I read *A Sand County Almanac*, Aldo Leopold, a dead white man I'd never heard of, from someplace I'd never been, sud-denly became an inspirational mentor. And so I set out to learn more about him: like how, as a forest ranger in the Southwest in the early 1900s, his conservation philosophy was sparked by the sight of a dying wolf he'd shot while deer hunting. He explained that hunters believed, then, that "fewer wolves meant more deer" and ultimately a "hunter's paradise." But the "fierce green fire" that Leopold watched fade from the doomed wolf's eyes would ignite the formation of what he called the Land Ethic—a way of thinking that "simply enlarges the boundaries of the community to include soils, waters, plants, and animals, or collectively: the land." Later he would see habitats devastated by hordes of hungry deer; over time, he came to understand that the balance between wolves and deer—predators and prey—was something to be revered and protected. Leopold's ideas evolved over the decades following the wolf's killing to crystallize in what is perhaps his seminal essay. In "Thinking Like a Mountain," he encouraged us to consider the whole ecosystem, and not tear it apart selfishly for our own ends. Love, Leopold said, was central to the Land Ethic.

Leopold went on to become a philosophizing professor of wildlife ecology at the University of Wisconsin, and most famously the owner of a burned-out farm near the city of Baraboo in one of Wisconsin's sand counties. There, he and his family converted an old chicken coop into a weekend cabin—the shack. In their time there, Leopold's family shared joyfully in nurturing the land back to health. The stories in *A Sand County Almanac* reminded me of the Home Place life I was already living. But there were other pleasures in the book, too. Leopold was obsessive about chronicling the seasons. He painted their nuances with words and in the process revealed a love for land that connected humankind to nature as a moral imperative. The ideas captured me. His writings were poetry more than prose, and they danced in my imagination. I was in love. The book would become sacred to me. It was my catalyst.

My brother influenced me in many ways, but we lived as adversaries for much of our time together on the Home Place. It was a brother vs. brother cold war with a seemingly impossible wall between us to breach. Jock always walked to the beat of a different—and very loud—drummer. While I was constantly in Daddy's shadow, hauling hay, cutting wood, fencing pastures, and doing anything else he required, Jock hung out with his white friends in "bad" places doing "bad" things.

He did not bend to authority readily. Fact is he hardly ever bent to it at all. Too smart to be compliant, Jock's always been an innovator. Besides the issues of *Playboy* in that room, there were copies of news and science magazines. Tacked to the wall was a star chart and always artwork—the twisted surrealism of Salvador Dali or an eye-tricking M. C. Escher print—clipped neatly out of a magazine. Jock sees things in a different way and maybe has a foot—or at least a part of his brain—in a different dimension. That was not something I always appreciated. I was a do-gooder and proudly so. Why couldn't Jock just be "good," too, like Mamatha and Daddy wanted him to be?

There were times when the three of us—Daddy, Jock, and I—worked together splitting wood or mending fences. I always wished for more. They were picture-perfect moments where we became the father and sons that I thought we should be. But those pictures were more often watercolors than oils, and faded with the inclement weather of stressful times. Jock disagreed openly with Daddy, sometimes *argued* with him. I couldn't fathom it. It was like arguing with God. And so I began to avoid him, the "bad" boy. He did likewise, probably seeing me in an equally disapproving light. We stopped talking. I began to think of myself as not even having a big brother. I don't remember saying goodbye when he left for college at Northeastern. For two to three years, there weren't ten words that passed between us.

During this time, I occasionally overheard tales of Jock's life in college. He spent lots of weekends hiking and camping in the mountains of New Hampshire. Later, after he transferred to Tennessee State University in Nashville, he bragged about how he'd challenged the rednecks by displaying a Confederate flag on his car. When he visited the Home Place, the smell of his cigarettes had changed. They had a greener scent that hung differently in the air. Jock openly voiced his opinion, slept in, and wandered alone. He owned his life in a way I couldn't imagine.

Jock's audacity has always amazed me. Sometimes it's shocked me. I secretly envied the ease with which he jumped the rails convention laid down. Many of the rules that I assumed absolute he questioned. The books Jock read, the music he listened to, the beat he marched to—they were all different. With thirty years of retrospect, I can now see that Mamatha's influence helped to set up this adversarial fraternal relationship. It was almost biblical. Mamatha told me better to stay away, and so I did. It would take Daddy's heart breaking to bring the two of us back together and make me realize that we had much more in common than not.

~

Bug

Julia is a fiercely loyal falcon who nurtures and defends—often at the expense of her own comfort and well-being. "Bug" (I'm not sure anyone really knows where the nickname came from) was often my protector and my mentor—as good a big sister as a little brother could ask for. More often than not what she had was shared with me.

Bug was as quiet and compliant as Jock was rebellious. Her hues and moods were subtler, like the muted greens that adorned her bedroom. That verdant room was a sanctum of mysterious girl secrets I was never privy to. But though I was invited into her space only a handful of times, I didn't make secret expeditions in there; we hardly spent any time in the house anyway. We lived much of our lives outside, thriving on dares and sometimes-questionable deeds. Competition defined our days. We'd race our bicycles, starting a quarter mile up the dirt road. She rode a sleek girlie bike with high handlebars, a banana seat, and a sissy bar. I was on my red-and-silver boy bike. With a tail of dust streaming behind us, Bug peddled hard and fast, even standing up to gain power. She almost always won. There were two-on-two basketball games, dirt-clod wars, and even stupid dares. In our quest to find out if a brass BB could really hurt, we went the direct route. With the muzzle of my little Daisy Cub rifle held at point-blank range, we took turns shooting one another in the ass. The yelps and howls confirmed it: yes, BBs might be tiny but they hurt like hell.

Beyond the BB affair, Bug encouraged the adventurer in me. There were all kinds of fun places to explore just outside our back door. Bug would pack a metal lunch box, one of the ones with cartoon characters or superheroes on the lid, with bologna sandwiches wrapped in wax paper and a mason jar full of super-sweet red Kool-Aid. A shady place under the big pines in front of the house or a spot beside the little ditch that we pretended was a stream became regular picnic spots. My big sister baked ginger-bread, tea cakes, and pizzas and shared them with everyone. Creating for others seemed like a joy. There was always some artsy-craftsy project in progress. Papier-mâché masks, collages from old magazines, copper-wire bracelets, and tie dye were all ripe media for Julia the artist.

Bug expanded my world beyond the Home Place, one clip-it-and-mail-it coupon at a time. She was the mail order princess. Once she ordered "amazing sea monkeys," which turned out to be anything but amazing. The comic book showed enticing pictures of half-monkey, half-mermaid beings frolicking in an aquarium para-dise. What kid could resist miniature simian mermaids! Bug saved nickels, dimes, and quarters for them; sent the order form away; and impatiently waited for her new pets to show up. The brine shrimp that finally arrived didn't look anything like the happy-go-lucky comic book characters that were supposed to come. Sea monkey fantasy deflated, it was on to the next thing; maybe selling vegetable seeds as a get-rich-quick road to summer wealth or buying some kit that always promised more than it delivered.

I wanted to hang out with Bug as much as I tried to avoid Jock. She was a protector, who occasionally buffered me from his assaults. She was a confidante I could tell about my girlfriends (or the girls I wanted to be my girlfriends). She was a chauffeur and chaperone in one, driving me to my first date when I was fifteen and conveniently running an errand to give me some time with my newfound lust interest. Bug taught me to drive and helped me develop a jump shot. I trusted her as I didn't anyone else.

Bug worked hard to earn little things on her own but what she wanted most she could not purchase or mail order. A different desire for independence burned inside Bug. Not the open rebellion that Jock blasted on hi-fi or the psychedelic push back of smoking and smut. She mostly followed the rules and did as she was told and never failed to get her chores done and school seemed easy for her. What Bug wanted most was a simple thing— basketball. My big sister was obsessed with hoops. She watched it on television; she played it all the time. The backboard on the barnside basket reverberated on many a summer's evening with the *thump-ba-bump* of layups and jump shots. If there'd been a net to swish, too, she would've burned up miles of nylon. Her turn-around jumper was silky smooth; her foul shots fell like rain; with her blowout Afro she looked like a superstar. Nancy Lieberman, one of the pioneers of women's professional basketball, was Bug's idol. She studied her every move and copied her form.

When I played against Bug I'd regularly get beaten. I was often outhustled, outjumped, and outscored. We played hard and I'd watch her confidence grow with each dribble and drive to the hoop, her hopes rising like hook shots on their way to two points. Practice after practice passed, with her ball skills sharpening to an edge that I was sure would make her successful. She'd ask me sometimes if I thought she was good enough. I can't remember ever thinking she wasn't. We'd laugh and talk about what it was going to be like when she made the team—or maybe even made it beyond high school.

But then Daddy always blocked her. Usually without explanation he would deny Bug's request to try out for the team. It disappointed her deeply. I think she wanted to give her best at something; to try to be someone different, someone great. But basketball was apparently not something Daddy thought women were supposed to do. Bug paid for his prejudice. It cut short her dreams.

Despite the fits and fights, disappointments and dreams way-laid, my sister Bug has remained true to who her birth status fated her to be: a caring nurturer seeking her own way. Over the years Bug has raised a daughter as a single mother, cared for terminally ill relatives, adopted abused pets, and become truer to herself. No, she never made the basketball team, but she's never ceased to be a star to me.

Jennifer

My little sister, Jennifer Mai, is a swallow—a flitting, wind-tossed bird. She is an impassioned, free-flying spirit. She came to the Ranch on the blooming of spring, a May flower, and the late-coming apple of Daddy's eye. She was someone to be treasured and protected. Six years' separation is an odd split between children. As the younger prepares to enter school for the first time, the elder is on the threshold of the turbulent teenage years. When her teenage trials came, I was out of the house.

Jennifer in many ways was almost a novelty to me; a Lanham "doll baby" who we only saw in the evenings and on weekends. While I stayed with Mamatha, Jennifer was cared for by a daytime nanny for one or two years and later on was shipped off to my Aunt Weesie's house in the town of Edgefield. Jennifer stayed there during the week, while I was still shuttling back and forth between the Ranch and Mamatha's and all of us were ferrying to Aiken for school. Jennifer and I were both semi-orphans for a while, living in two worlds. The last Lanhams born to the Home Place were household hybrids.

And so in many ways our contact and bonding came later on—and is still developing. The first fertile ground ever plowed between us came when she was ten and I was sixteen. I was a new driver and volunteered to take her to a friend's birthday party. I had ulterior motives. While Jennifer was being entertained by birthday cake and balloons, I would make my way to a girlfriend's house to partake of kisses and flesh fondling. My sixteen-year-old hormonal brain was working all the angles.

On the day our first real bonds were sealed, one of the winter storms that throws ice and snow way south had come through. Within a day or two most of it had melted away and the way was safe for the twenty-minute drive to Trenton. Jennifer, in her pigtail twists, was giddy to get to the cake and ice cream. Mama, not quite a year widowed, was pleased with my helping hand but had warned me, as a greenhorn driver, about the back roads that might still be covered in black ice. I promised to be careful—but was distracted by other priorities.

Everything seemed fine on the way. The snow and ice that had crippled the area just days before was only visible in the cool of the woodland shadows. My head buzzing with thoughts of the rendez-vous to come, I pushed the '69 VW Beetle into high gear and sped confidently past Miller's store, turning right onto a roughly paved road that snaked through the piney woods. With the shortcut I would cut at least ten minutes off the longer route. Although my license was new, I'd been driving for a couple of years on dirt roads and felt a little like Mario Andretti or Richard Petty as I dipped in and out of the curves. It felt good to be free.

I was making record time. But only five minutes or so from our final destination I nosed the Beetle into a sharp curve and the world dove into a sudden spin. Things went around and around— sky, trees, sky, trees—and then everything stopped. I was no longer looking at the road ahead or thinking of the pleasures to come. The windshield was filled with grass and mud. The Beetle was resting, nose down, in a ditch on the side of the road.

Jennifer was frozen in her seat—wide eyed and quietly sitting as if nothing had happened. Luckily she'd been buckled in securely, but was she in shock? I asked if she was OK. She nodded affirmatively. We got out of the car and surveyed the situation. "Shit! Damn!" I cursed aloud. It was probably the first time Jennifer had ever heard those words. I was in big trouble. I had failed in a responsibility and the cause was clearly my selfish adolescent agenda. The car was stuck in a ditch and we weren't where we were supposed to be. I had no way of contacting anyone to help us. Things looked really bad.

The little section of road, still darkly shaded at noon, was cov-ered in the black ice I'd been warned about. The cursing didn't stop. Jennifer just stood there, pigtails still perfectly in order, not knowing what, if anything, to say. I was not yet in full panic mode but I was getting there. This was not a heavily traveled route, and there was barely anyone who actually lived on it. The chance of anybody coming by to help us was small. Maybe if I walked back toward the crossroads I could flag someone down to help us.

Just as I decided that the walk was the only option, a pickup truck, sitting high on big knobby tires, appeared from around the curve. It was one of those loud, rumbling redneck trucks, a Confederate-flag license plate on the front bumper and a mud-splattered paint job indicating a lot of time off-road. I was old enough to think the worst and knew that the stars and bars didn't usually precede folks who were black-people friendly. I saw the situation getting worse. The truck slowed to a stop and a window came down.

"Ya'll need some help?" a man drawled.

Surprised and relieved, I watched as the two men from the truck winched the little car from the ditch like it was a toy. The bumper was slightly twisted and part of the hood was covered with red clayey mud, snow, and pine straw. But when I cranked the engine it turned over, none the worse for wear. I thanked the men for their help and offered to pay them the few dollars I had in my pocket. They refused and rumbled off. We'd been delivered—by the people I would've least expected to help.

Jennifer and I got back in the car and continued on to the party. I went through the checklist again. "Are you sure you're OK?" With a pigtail-bouncing nod, she assured me that she was. I then asked her a question, equal in importance—at least to my physical well-being. "Are you gonna tell Mama?"

"Not if you don't want me to, I won't," she said. And then, per-haps in the most genuine moment that she and I have ever shared, she followed, unsolicited, with the two words of bond: "I promise." She's kept that word for over thirty years.

⁓

And me? I'm third in line, sharing a middler role with Bug. I make my self-identification in the mirror every morning, taking stock of the ursine-eyed, chubby-cheeked guy staring back. I'm the hermit thrush of the flock—a brown-backed shadow hugger who prefers the world's darker, quieter recesses, with an occasional foray into the light. I'm no singer but I sling words every now and again to express what my heart feels. There's a little of each of us in one another. And in that way I am my siblings—and they are me.

We are all, the Hoover and Willie May Lanham brood, a familial diaspora, cast apart by time and circumstance but connected to a land legacy that is also fragmented and failing. Negligence is the sea that separates us from some greater reconnection. There are still rifts of misunderstanding, too. Jock holds onto his seven acres on the Home Place—the only tether actively binding black Lanham name to Edgefield land—but I visit him too infrequently. The rest of us—Julia, Jennifer, and I—have wishes and wants but have not acted to reclaim the past. I want to hear bobwhite calling and watch white-tailed deer feeding in a bean field again; I dream that somehow the legacy will not be completely swallowed up by time and trees. My siblings' wishes are likely different but if I could somehow cross the seas that separate us—if I could guide us back to those fields—I would do it. If somehow we could link our names to Lanham land again it would be worth the effort.

First-Sunday God

Some keep the Sabbath going to Church—
I keep it, staying at Home—
With a Bobolink for a Chorister—
And an Orchard, for a Dome.

— Emily Dickinson

MY RELIGIOUS ODYSSEY BEGAN WITH A CRUCIFIX AND A fascination with Communion. After Mama and Daddy inexplicably decided that I needed to attend Catholic kindergarten—although we weren't Catholic ourselves—I ended up in a room full of six-year-olds under the strict and sometimes painful tutelage of a Sister Somebody. Her authority was absolute. Like other kindergartners, we learned letters, numbers, and silly songs. But I also learned that following instruction to the letter was critical to remaining pain free.

One day I decided to color a picture of a little boy brown. Why shouldn't the pale outline be made to look like me? There was a whole box of crayons to use, after all. A wooden ruler rapped across one's knuckles, however, can be a strong persuader in the hands of the divinely inspired. I'm not sure the brown crayon received much further consideration during my kindergarten career.

The Sister's punishment didn't do much to dampen my spirits, though. I loved Catholicism. I became smitten with the ceremonial traditions of the rosary and Communion. And then there were all those mumbled words that seemed to mean something important. I looked forward to the end of recess because that meant we'd all crowd into the chapel, where a man in robes would intone the words I never really understood and then drink something out of a huge golden cup. Whatever was in the cup—and I imagined it to be the sweetest, reddest Kool-Aid ever—I wanted some. To achieve this, I would need to become like all the other people I saw drinking from the cup.

Mama's vision for my St. Gerard school picture was for her little brown Drew to sit up straight and tall in a crisp white turtleneck, with a broad smile for the camera. That wasn't quite what I had in mind. I insisted on wearing a navy-blue jacket over my sweater that morning. Mama agreed, with the stipulation that I remove the coat before I sat for the picture. I disobeyed. With my jacket layered on top of the turtleneck, I looked just like the collared, golden-cup-swigging men. They would have no choice but to invite me up front to partake of the holy Kool-Aid. I was pleased— the chubby-cheeked, all-knowing smile in the picture proves it. I'd also taken to mumbling chants, saying Hail Marys, and throwing crosses across my chest the way I saw the nuns and priests doing. It was all coming together nicely. Mama and Daddy were less than thrilled. The next year the conservative confines of black Baptist Christianity would banish any thoughts of Catholicism from my young mind. It would be fire, brimstone, cheap wine from tiny glasses, and cracker-crumb Communion from that point forward.

With Catholicism in the ideological rearview I was ripe for fundamentalist indoctrination. For the next six or seven years I was under constant surveillance and training. Becoming Baptist would require some hammering on my improperly bent soul, and

Mamatha was the person to do it. God and the Baptist Church were the underpinning of her being. Mystical things could happen at any time, but on Sunday, magic moved over for miracles. Sunday was God's day and that meant church, prayer, the Bible, and being saved and sanctified in the Holy Spirit.

Mamatha called on that spirit every day, morning, noon, and night. She insisted that I do the same. Fearing some biblical calamity befalling me—a lightning bolt striking out of a clear blue sky or being turned into a pillar of salt if I looked at the wrong thing—I was obedient. I was constantly terrified that something bad was going to happen because God judged me unworthy at that moment. And with all the "shalt nots" and "lest thous" that filled the Bible Mamatha made me read aloud, I was certain that I was always in violation of some commandment.

"God is a jealous God!" Mamatha would say. I couldn't quite figure that one out: God jealous? But with His quick temper and tendency to let loose plagues, part seas, and promise destruction by fire the next time, who wouldn't be afraid of Him?

"Fear God!" she'd say. "Put all yo' trust in the Lawd, baby." She promised that if I became "born again," "washed in the blood," "waded in the water," that all would be forgiven. And so when my parents, who weren't anywhere near as zealous as my grandmother was, left home for a week on an educational expedition, Mamatha's indoctrination was intense.

That was a week of almost constant prayer during the day and revival in the evenings, with Jeter Baptist Church full of people staring straight through my soul. I listened as the preacher delivered earsplitting, soul-stirring sermons about eternal damnation, the evil that controls us all like puppets, and how thinking something bad was the same as doing it. What? God was in my head, too? I had to have some kind of insurance against the misery that was waiting for my sinful little brown soul. Fear and my grandmother's less-than-subtle insistence sent me to the front of the church one evening to confess my desire for salvation.

I told the preacher in the most earnest and God-fearing tone that I could muster that I wanted to be saved; I would forevermore be the best boy possible, in obedient and faithful service to God. The congregation sitting in the shadows of the dimly lit sanctuary unanimously cheered. A chorus of "Amen!," "Thank ya Jesus!," and "Praise the Lawd!" let me know I had done the right thing. I took my place on the "mourner's bench," the front pew marked for newly saved souls. I didn't feel so safe up there, though; my soul was suddenly naked before God and all those people. Mamatha stood at the rear of the church in her starched white usher uniform. Stooped as always but spiritually upright, she was smiling. Her mission had been successful. I was going to heaven! A chorus of cicadas and katydids, unimpressed, droned outside the spiritual spectacle.

The final formalization of my blood pact with Jesus would have to take place underwater. Being a creature of the woods, I never met a ditch, puddle, or pool I could resist. Water was always a draw for me, even if it was only a few inches sitting in a road rut after a rain. In an algae-stained cement pond, underneath the watchful gaze of what I hoped was a forgiving god, I was dunked in the dingy waters of redemption. The little black commas of tadpoles swam around in the murkiness, waiting—maybe praying—to be frogs. The baptism was the final sealing of my promise to be good, forever. And yet by the time of my watery communion with the little amphibians-to-be, my acceptance of the alleged loving kindness of

God had grown less certain. It had felt good on the night I pledged myself to salvation but now I was feeling guilty. I'd fooled God and my grandmother into believing something I wasn't so sure I believed myself. I emerged from the born-again bath gasping for breath but not really feeling any different. Beyond my sputtering intake of some of the algae- and amphibian-flavored baptismal tea, I didn't feel infused with anything, least of all the presence of God.

I tried to hide the lies with dutifulness. That meant sitting in a place where I never saw God or even once felt the presence of love, grace, and mercy that was supposed to accompany Him. Back in those days, most of the black country churches rotated Sunday services. Jeter was a first-Sunday church. Because of this once-a-month structure, the service was a marathon, where four weeks' praise, prayer, preaching, and redemption were crammed into you in one go. For three hours or more, a span of time that passed glacially, I would have to sit and listen to someone tell me how evil I was and what terrible punishment was in store if I didn't repent. My five-second swim with the tadpoles had been just an entry fee to salvation; Satan would follow me for the rest of my life, tempting me with things I'd better turn away from or else. I owed God a debt of obedience and guilt that I could never repay. That realization, even as a prepubescent boy, set hard on me.

I hated first Sundays then. Later on I came to hate most Sundays, because they caged my mind, body, and soul into four walls. I couldn't look beyond my physical discomfort to see that going to church was a kind of social glue. Black folks and church in the South are stuck fast together like cockleburs on a dog's back. Church for black folk has always been the escape from a week of toil, a place of refuge where the community's news can be shared. Sunday was one

of the few days we might call our own. Back then, though, all I knew
was that I hated going to church.

Sunday always felt different. Sometimes in good ways: I got to
eat breakfast at the Ranch and Mama usually made grits and gravy
or salmon patties. At Sunday meals we said the Lord's Prayer—arts,
thous, and "not trespassing against"—rather than the abbreviated
and efficient "God is great, God is good," get-it-over-and-done-
with-so-we-can-eat appeal. We read the Bible on Sunday mornings,
a few verses to confirm the Sabbath.

The Bible and biscuits were fine. Breakfasts followed by some
time wandering in wildness would've been perfect. Running out
to contemplate the transformation of tadpoles or the dizzy-defying
dances of whirligig beetles in some muddy puddle would have
been worship enough in my mind.

But on far too many Sundays I was pulled from the roaming rhythm and natural worship that truly fulfilled me. A church
Sunday meant that God was suddenly confined to something that
seemed much less miraculous than the woods and fields where
creation was so evident. Inside the church's walls the wind didn't
blow and bobwhite quail didn't call, the hawks didn't soar and creeks
didn't gurgle. Instead I was supposed to find peace with pictures of
a long-haired, fair-skinned Jesus staring at me and a man I didn't
know hollering that the world would end if I didn't behave better.
Even the ritual of donning the church uniform—a stiffly starched
shirt; a clip-on tie; and a fun-constraining, play-inhibiting, better-
keep-it-clean, double-knit polyester suit of armor, along with the
inflexible, hard-soled shoes that wouldn't let me run away—led me
to believe that God would only accept me on a very limited basis.
Well-worn jeans and hole-riddled T-shirts weren't good enough for
Him. With the suits always too tight and the services always too

long, God seemed somehow far, far away, and not someone I really wanted to know.

Jeter still stands where it did when I was imprisoned there—not far from Ropers Crossroads and a stone's throw from Miller's store, where we used to buy little brown paper bags full of penny candy, pinwheel cookies, and ice-cold RC Colas and Upper 10 sodas. Jeter is just ten minutes from the Home Place and stuck back in the woods, like most everything in my world was. It was like my grandmother's place, a throwback, a functional antiquity that belonged in a different place and time. Hard-as-stone pews offered little comfort to a squirming behind. The heart-pine wooden floors echoed with the rhythmic footbeats of worshippers. There were no hymnals. Instead the songs were "lined," read by an old deacon during the devotional service: "Hymn number 23, common meter—Must Jesus bear the cross alone, and all the world go free? No, there's a cross for everyone, and there's a cross for me!" The congregation would obediently pick up the verse and a hundred voices would blend in a harmony rooted in something deeper than first Sunday. There was no piano or organ to hold the tune. Just the imprint of decades of singing, born of a time when only a privileged few could read and only the thump of feet kept the rhythm.

There was no air-conditioning in the church for a long time. That meant that it was hot, sometimes hellishly so. The place where Jesus and his angry father lived to help me get into paradise wasn't even comfortable. The pictures on the church fans—Martin Luther King Jr.'s intensely kind gaze; the detached but perfectly poised (and suspiciously white) praying hands; and my favorite, the perfect little white country church nestled in autumn splendor—were minor but welcome distractions that helped to pass the hours. Was there another tortured, starving black boy, I wondered, sitting in the perfect little church, forever imprisoned in the fan's flat dimensions? Surely it was cooler in there. The leafy riot of red and yellow framing the little chapel looked like October should feel. I could imagine the frosty morning, smell the ripening season, hear the honking geese overhead. Were the brilliant colors of the leaves against the perfect blue sky what heaven looked like? I hoped so. I dreamed of that place. Not the little church—or even heaven—but the brilliant landscape and the wild perfection that surrounded it. My God lived out there.

Inevitably, the church-fan fantasy would end, when I had to stand for this song or that prayer. Sit and daydream. Stand and sing. Sit and daydream. Stand and pray. And so many Sundays went. I myself prayed for it to be over. Heaven, the preacher bellowed, was a faraway place, its golden streets flowing with creamy milk and sticky-sweet honey. In hell, people gnashed their teeth and tore at their own flesh. While heaven sounded interesting and hell downright horrifying, I simply preferred dusty dirt roads and Mama's fried chicken. The man of God's fervent, frothing delivery guaranteed that there would be no white-tailed deer or stealthy foxes in paradise. His yelling would've scared them off.

The years at Jeter etched things both good and bad onto the blank slate of my childhood. This was old-time religion, salvation at the hands of a blue-eyed God who wielded the Bible like a whip. I wonder if, when I stepped into that slimy baptismal pool and invaded the tadpoles' universe, they thought that I was some gigantic black amphibian god come to deliver them from the restrictions of their stagnant, confining world. Did they fear me, waiting to be smote down because of some larval transgression, or did they welcome my sudden appearance, praising the clouds passing above for their salvation? When they changed to four-legged hopping beings and escaped the pool, was the next world what they thought it would be?

~

I had turned against the first-Sunday God. Growing up in an atmosphere where learning was a family value, the preacher's sermons, which frequently dismissed education as ungodly, seemed odd to me even at an early age. No books were tossed or burned but there weren't many being opened and read either. The repression felt heavy, like late-August heat. Sometimes it was hard to breathe.

The breaking point came at a church conference—one of those rare occasions beyond the fire-and-brimstone slinging, where people were actually supposed to get together, think, and make decisions. Much of the Lanham family was in attendance. Mama, Daddy, Jock, Bug, and I—along with Mamatha, aunts, uncles, some cousins, and all the past Lanhams in the overgrown graveyard—sat in the swelter of a summer evening in the dimly lit church. The meeting was convened to decide the fate of the new preacher, who'd come to the church only a couple of years before. Reverend Adams wasn't a malingerer. There was no affair, no hidden sexuality, and no thievery. Yet the issues were serious, the complaints constant, and the accusations stinging. The new preacher had brought something obscene to Jeter's table: the *Living Bible*, a plainly worded version of the King James. Blasphemy! That "thous" and "thees" would be replaced by "yous" and "mes" was anathema.

Beyond the issues with the Bible, there was the preaching. The hollering, screaming, guilt-filled, hell-bound sermons of the old-guard preacher had been replaced by calmer tones and a lot less condemnation. To add insult to injury, Reverend Adams had demanded that education be a centerpiece of the church's mission. He talked not only of "reading, writing, and 'rithmetic," but of college and careers beyond the mills and menial labor that many in our congregation seemed destined for. At odds were a complacent slave mentality of putting one's fate blindly in God's hands, and using a divinely inspired brain to think and follow a bright star to freedom and something better.

The night of the inquisition was hot, inside and out. If the stars were shining to enlighten, their glow failed to find the attendees who shrouded themselves in the ignorance that fell with the dusk. The droning cicadas didn't drown out the rancor of the calls for redress. The sweat rolled off anger-furrowed brows, voices were raised, and fingers were pointed accusingly. The deacons of the church rose one by one to explain why the new pastor had to go: he was ungodly and unfit, putting school, self-determination, and thinking ahead of faith in God. My parents and a few others rose, too, in defense of education and the new way.

I sat there with little knowledge of what it all really meant but with the full understanding that grown-ups were very mad with one another and that God was supposedly somewhere in the middle of it all. Eventually someone birthed a bastardized version of parliamentary procedure and a vote was quickly cast. I raised my hand, shadowing my parents and a few others, but it didn't matter. Jeter Baptist Church dismissed Reverend Adams. Night is never as dark as when one refuses to shine a lantern to see. Hoover and Willie May left Jeter that night with us in tow, and never returned.

I was secretly giddy. The exodus meant no more marathon worship services or being trapped in polyester on rock-hard pews—at least for a bit. Mama and Daddy tried different churches on and off. We visited Tabernacle, the sophisticated big-city church in

Augusta, with stained glass windows and a tall steeple. Important black people attended Tabernacle and sometimes the services were even broadcast on television. It didn't stick, though; most Sundays after the exodus were spent pleasantly and lazily at home. I could read the funny pages and roam the woods without worry.

My grandmother lamented the leaving, feeling as if we'd turned our backs on the religious roots that anchored us to God. "It hurts me to my heart," she said, to pass her home church on the way to worship somewhere else. So we ferried her back and forth to Jeter but never attended a Sunday service there ourselves. I suppose Mama and Daddy felt that there was something more important in faith than a simple allegiance to tradition, and so we left the spiritual bondage of Jeter behind and made our way through a wilderness of sorts, until we found Canaan.

⁓

Mt. Canaan Baptist Church was the first founded by Reverend Alexander Bettis almost a century earlier. Bettis was a black Moses: he grew up a slave, but once freed bound himself to the idea that learning was the straightest road to liberty. Trained to read but not to write, his half literacy didn't quell his ambition; the former slave became the first ordained black pastor in a four-county region. Along the way he established a string of churches and a boarding school that educated hundreds and influenced thousands. Bettis Academy, which my father attended, became a beacon for black Americans searching for enlightenment. With education built on barter—classes were given in exchange for sacks of flour or labor on the twenty-seven-acre campus—a number of leaders emerged from Biddle Hall and the sandy Trenton campus.

Jeter was an offspring of Bettis, too, but somewhere between its founding and the upheaval we witnessed, the cultures of the two churches had diverged dramatically. It was as if the ecology of the places where the two churches stand had infused into the institutions themselves. Mt. Canaan sits in the sand of an ancient coastal plain where longleaf pine prospers. Jeter is mired northward in red clay and rolling piedmont hills. Maybe the sticky clay gummed up the minds of the Jeter folks over the years, like it did the roots of green things looking for something more to grow in. Perhaps the sandy soil of Mt. Canaan allowed the thoughts of the Canaanites to sift and shift like water and nutrients through the looser consolidation. The differences between the two places were obvious even to me, a child whose mind had been taught to measure godliness by the hours spent sitting and listening to the spread of ignorance and condemnation.

Mt. Canaan was a second- and fourth-Sunday church. Initially I wasn't excited about twice as much praying and pew time but the services at Mt. Canaan were half as long as those at Jeter. Things were newer and more modern there, too. Carpeted floors, piano and organ music, and a program schedule that was closely followed made it seem like we'd been thrown into some future world. And then there was actual learning. Instead of the one-room-schoolhouse mentality that treated knowledge as an afterthought or worse, at Mt. Canaan there were age-specific classes meeting in separate rooms with books and materials to share and learn from. Best of all, the preacher didn't scream or condemn. It didn't seem to be a part of his Sunday repertoire or a part of the church's culture.

The period of enlightenment that came from finding Mt. Canaan was like a gap opening in the densest of forests, liberating seeds long suppressed to sprout up in new light. Daddy was immediately accepted, like some sort of prodigal son. I don't think any fattened calves were sacrificed but there was more than enough Lanham-family adulation to feast on. Beyond the older folks who had known Daddy Joe and his reputation as a farmer, teacher, and principal, there were people who knew Daddy from his Bettis Academy days as a stellar student and athlete.

Within a short time, Daddy was teaching Sunday school and before long was elevated to Sunday school superintendent. Mama threw herself fully into things, joining the choir and the Willing Workers Club, and eventually rising to deaconess and full-fledged Canaanite.

Jock and Bug were figuring out things for themselves, past the point where any preacher could influence them. They attended church sporadically and for the most part weren't forced to go. But all those years of my grandmother grinding God into me took hold of my psyche in insidious ways, leaving church something I could not skip without a lot of internal bickering. At least Mt. Canaan made the brainwashing more palatable.

At Jeter, children were usually commanded to be seen and never heard. But at Mt. Canaan, there were scouting, summer, and music programs, outings and trips to places Jeter would never have taken me or encouraged me to go. I made friends. There was a whole crèche of kids my age to grow up and hang out with. There were nurturing people everywhere, willing to help in so many ways. Jeter was fading into the memory of my young life.

Sometimes we learn how to be by observing people we don't want to be like. I owe Jeter and Mt. Canaan equal shares in who I am. Jeter is still inextricably tangled up in the roots of my family tree. Daddy Joe, Mamatha, and some of their children lie moored in the dirt there, nourishing the trees that somehow find a way to pierce the tightly grained soils. I hold onto a few fond memories of church suppers under the big oaks, where the greasy, hunger-enticing aromas of fried chicken, macaroni and cheese, and pound cakes made the marathon wait through all the singing, preaching, and praying occasionally worthwhile.

Even education snuck in sometimes. On Children's Day and Easter we all had speeches to recite. There were kids who chose simple two-line poems to remember; it was cute and low pressure. Mama, always the ambitious matron, insisted on more rigorous recitations: Rudyard Kipling, Robert Frost, Robert Louis Stevenson. She'd choose poems that were much longer than everyone else's for us to memorize and recite. Still, I had a perfect recitation record until she chose a forty-line Henry Wadsworth Longfellow poem called "The Children's Hour." I set about trying to learn it on the Saturday night before. Needless to say, on the day of reckoning, when my name was called to summon me forward—I failed. I got halfway through and froze in forgetfulness. I stumbled over fragments of verse and then sat down to a smattering of sympathetic applause. Mama's polite but tight-lipped smile was enough to let me know she wasn't pleased. I sat and stewed. Other kids marched to the front and some of them failed just like I had. That relieved some of the pressure. As my misery gained company the possibilities of a fussing out or whipping faded. Black cherry ice cream was served after the program and it was fine medicine for forgetfulness. The food and family gathering made it seem almost—*almost*—unlike church.

Mostly, though, Jeter taught me what God wasn't—or shouldn't—be. And for that lesson I will always be thankful.

Mt. Canaan also twined itself into my family tree, but it found a way to encourage growth instead of strangling it. The God there was someone I didn't mind knowing, mostly. Time at Mt. Canaan was spent not bowing under a chastening rod but being uplifted by kind hands and hearts that saw something beyond a heaven to wait for.

I visited Jeter on a couple of later occasions, to help bear my grandmother's casket and watch two of her daughters retired to the family burial plots near the edge of the encroaching forest. There were few familiar faces—most of the old guard had long since passed on—but I saw some vague resemblances in those who came after. I did not know them, however, nor did they know me. And while the clay there is still red and sticky and the building remains much the same, the church's attitude now wasn't something I could assess in the couple-hour span of a few funerals. I hear not much has changed.

Mama is still a member of Mt. Canaan and has been a key factor in its success over the past forty years. She led efforts to restore portions of the Bettis Academy campus and the legacy of the former slave turned educator. For decades the drive to save and resurrect the place that launched so many in the Mt. Canaan community into prominence has kept Mama busy with a labor of love. There are MDs, PhDs, and a lot of other letters behind people's names that speak to accomplishment borne of the church off Highway 25. This success is what Alexander Bettis might have pictured when he laid the first foundation stone and insisted that learning be a sacred thing.

Even though I cherished most of my time there, Mt. Canaan also fell off the list of places I visit when I return to Edgefield. It's not because of a loss of affection or appreciation for the people there but because I've had to move on. Depending on the day I claim different labels spiritually. They run the gamut from atheist to Zen. I'm not sure any of them really matter. What does matter: I've expanded the walls of my spiritual existence beyond the pews and pulpit to include longleaf savannas, salt marshes, cove forests, and tall-grass prairie. The miracles for me are in migratory journeys and moonlit nights. Swan song is sacred. Nature seems worthy of worship.

Fledgling

Little Brown Icarus

In Honor of the Tuskegee Airmen
"Because of their heroic action . . . they were called
Schwartze Vogelmenschen (Black Bird Men) . . ."

— Tuskegee Airmen Memorial,
Walterboro, South Carolina

THE GROUND LOOKED MILES AWAY. JUST MOMENTS BEFORE, I'D
been standing on the neatly mown front yard of the Ranch, looking
up. I did that a lot—look up. Bug and I used to ride in the backseat
of our Ford Fairlane, looking up at the sky reflected in a mirror we
held angled just so. As we traveled home from school we watched
the wild blue yonder whiz by. It was like flying through space while
bound securely by the safety of sturdy steel walls and the comfort
of a sticky-hot vinyl seat. Sometimes when Daddy sped over a little
hill or around a sharp curve, there was even a momentary fluttery
feeling of weightlessness, tickling my toes and crawling quickly up
through my stomach.

But right now, there was no car to confine me, no mirror to
turn the world upside down. It was just me and the clouds speeding by on the stratosphere's highway. I'd climbed way up here—up
the wobbly wooden ladder that seemed a hundred feet high—to be
that much closer to those clouds. The blades of grass that a moment
before had pressed prickly, soft, and cool between my toes now
melded into a distant green mat, no longer so inviting from the van-
tage of twelve feet. I might as well have been on Mount Everest.

From this height the whole world lay stretched out before me. The fresh scent of new-cut grass soaked the air. Mama worked in the Ranch kitchen canning jelly and blanching tomatoes. Daddy wrestled with the mechanical mule, churning up new ground with the rototiller to make the garden grow. Twittering barn swallows swooped in and out of the hay shed. Grazing black cows dotted the pasture. The deep dark woods lay all around with God knows what watching from the shadows. What I could see, hear, smell, and imagine all came into focus up there. I sat in that crow's nest and thought hard about what I was going to do. Caught between the fear of falling and the pride of not surrendering to that fear, I counted down—

10 . . . 9 . . . 8 . . . 7 . . .

Mission control stand by!

6 . . . 5 . . . 4 . . .

I closed my eyes—

3 . . . 2 . . . 1 . . .

—and launched myself into the summer air. There was the briefest sensation that I'd finally beaten gravity. Unbound by earth or the ladder's last rung, for a moment I was flying free, hanging in space. That is, until my old nemesis grabbed me by the ankles and threw my chunky brown body back to the soft green mat that hid a very hard ground. Hitting feetfirst and rolling to absorb the sudden jolt back to flightlessness, I came to rest, looking up, in the same prickly blades of grass that had bidden me farewell before I climbed up the launchpad. Back on terra firma and mostly without injury I was happy that courage had prevailed. I reveled in the millisecond of cloud-like freedom, untethered from any binding force. Newton's math reveals that I was "free" for less than a second, but it had seemed like much longer.

The episode was repeated many times. I launched myself from trees, roofs, and haystacks. No matter how hard I tried, though, I couldn't fly. Mary Poppins and Wile E. Coyote had lied to me. Umbrellas didn't float me gently to the ground and no matter how vigorously I flapped my cardboard wings, my husky weight fell back to earth—always awkwardly and often painfully. No matter how fast or far I ran before my attempts, the ground was always there too quickly. Until the day I discovered swing-flying, I was convinced that gravity had it in for me personally.

But the swing was the thing. Kicking the ground to leverage myself into pendulous motion and pumping my legs rhythmically— back and forth, back and forth—I found the world swishing by in an ever-widening arc of almost airborne joy. Tenuously restrained from the full freedom of flight by just two spindly chains, swinging was adrenaline-fueled fun. Up and down, back and forth, higher and higher until just before the forward peak of the cycle, when I let go of the chains and gave myself over to momentum. Uncoupled, I was launched skyward, finally finding the way up instead of down. With arms waving and legs flailing, and somehow believing that any small movement might keep me up just a moment longer, it was as close as I ever got to free flying. And then I was on the ground looking up—wishing—again.

I was a caramel-colored Icarus with a hard head, persisting in the fantasy that flying was something I was meant to do. While the word "aerodynamic" never crossed my lips or my mind at the age of ten, the elementary principles of flight were not lost on me. Run faster—increase thrust; shed the shirt—decrease drag; flap cardboard wings—increase lift. Swing higher, harder, faster. Eat less jelly cake and decrease weight. Nothing worked.

I watched birds fly, flutter, hover, soar, and sail through the air. Why should they have so much fun? How could something as fragile as a feather mean so much? I'd picked up lots of them— large, small, and of many colors—on rambles through the woods and fields. Azure-hued blue jay feathers, white tipped and barred with black to advertise bravado; dirty-brown "buzzard" feathers, big, stiff, and strong; tawny-brown barred owl feathers, softened on the edges for silence. I marveled at the silky smoothness of their contours and sometimes stuck them in my nappy little Afro, pretending to be part American Indian. I clutched handfuls of feathers in my sweaty hands and ran like the wind but I never became the bird I wanted to be. If desire had meant flight I would've soared like an eagle.

$\sim$

Flight was my first fascination. I didn't understand why birds didn't have to worship the same god of always falling down that I did. If you watch a bird in flight, you'll feel an instinctual wondering, a questioning of how. Whether it be a pigeon's strong direct line to push home through a canyon of glass and concrete, a hunting hawk's faithful float over a fallow field, or a hummingbird's miraculous hover in the search for sweet sustenance, the astounding potential of a feather's lift cannot be ignored.

The feathers were special treasures fallen from the sky, tokens thrown earthward by heavenly beings. I discovered that if I held one of those gifts from a vulture or turkey out a speeding car's window, it always wanted to go up. Even when I ran with them in my hands I could feel the tiny forces of lift that made flight possible. All the feathers on a wing, together, made the magic happen.

There were other flying things that called. Bats intrigued me.

Universal kid knowledge suggested that they were really just rats with wings, and could turn into bloodsucking vampires at night. Everyone claimed that bats' primary mission in life was to entangle themselves in women's hair. But I marveled at the erratic fluttering flight that took them about the yard on a summer evening. I wondered how they flew without feathers.

There was a huge mimosa tree in the backyard. It exploded with cotton candy–like flowers in the summertime, drawing in a kaleidoscope of butterflies. A mélange of winged color danced about the pink profusion of blooms. I caught butterflies occasionally, not with a net but by simply sneaking up on them as they fed and quickly and gently grabbing their wings between my thumb and forefinger when they closed. Tiger swallowtails, monarchs, and many more species that I didn't know came under my close scrutiny. Sometimes the captive would unfurl its coiled-up tongue and tickle my palm for a salty taste of sweat. Bats and butterflies and birds: all of them blessed with wings, and me stuck in the soil with two arms and ten fingers.

Looking even higher skyward, I saw another way up. It wouldn't require me to shape-shift or somehow evolve beyond my present form. Tiny Piper Cubs flew the countryside, often directly over the Home Place, inspecting the gas-pipeline right-of-way. They might dip their wings if I waved hard and long enough. Further above, little silver airplanes left cloudy trails across the blue.

I would be a pilot. While I waited to grow up, I lived the imaginary life of a combat ace. I flew by plastic-model proxy. Saving quarters and the occasional dollars earned doing chores I bought and assembled kit after kit of model airplanes, mostly World War II–era fighters like Mustangs, Thunderbolts, Spitfires, Focke-Wulfs, and Zeros. I read everything I could about them and watched every single grainy documentary of combat footage. I dreamed of wearing a leather flight helmet and goggles while pushing the propeller-driven machines through the skies.

Once the box full of parts became a plane, I'd fly the miniature warbirds around the house, zooming in and out of skyscapes bounded by Formica countertops, kitchen tables, and easy chairs. Nothing was safe. I strafed housecats and toy trains. I perfected aerial maneuvers—split Ss, power dives, and barrel rolls—over unnamed shag-carpeted countries and flew in hundreds of sorties through every room of the house. I downed enemy fighters, protected armadas of B-17 Flying Fortresses, and almost single-handedly made the world safe for democracy. And in all of my imaginings I was white, like all of the daring, ace fighter pilots the documentaries ever showed with thumbs up as they sallied off on another heroic mission. But although none of the television or books I saw while building my career as a plastic-model ace showed it, there were people with black and brown skin who'd lived my dream and flown through the flak-ridden skies of World War II Europe.

Those pilots were the Tuskegee Airmen. They flew the real versions of the airplanes I played with: Airacobras, Warhawks, and the "Queen of the Sky"—the P-51 Mustang fighter. Against all odds they overcame racism at home in the United States and endured substandard treatment by the military to become heroes. Brash and brave, they painted the tails of their Thunderbolts and Mustangs bright red to distinguish their unit. After battling the brass for time in combat they proved to everyone that they belonged. Their effectiveness in protecting the streams of heavy bombers against German-fighter attacks was exemplary. The "Red Tails" fought with distinction, just like Daddy Joe and the 371st had in World War I. I wonder—if I'd known of them back then, would my dreams have come true?

I can't look at a red-tailed hawk aloft on a thermal and not think of those heroes who came before. Maybe some of them were inspired by feathered flying things like I was. Even the airmen's enemies, fighting for a supposed "super-race," marveled at the colored fliers, calling them "black bird men."

I wasn't quite a man when I put away the childish things, but I was old enough to understand that unassisted flight wasn't going to happen for me, no matter how hard I flapped or how high I jumped. Dreams of fame as a fighter pilot eventually faded, too, as my identity and desires evolved. But while many things in my mind changed, the fascination with birds and flight stuck hard and fast.

Birds were a part of everyday life on the Home Place. There were the blue jays that "stole" Mamatha's pecans in the fall. There were the turkeys that gobbled in the spring, and the quail that called in the summer. There were flocks of sparrows and juncos that seemed grateful for the grits Mamatha scattered in the snow.

I've noticed birds for as long as I can remember. Mamatha's seed-spreading sympathy for the snowbirds in the winter was the first I ever knew of anyone feeding birds. Daddy's cornfield confrontations with crows—and his practice of killing one and hanging it to scare away the other marauders—worked. Crows were anything but birdbrained. Hoover understood that the big black birds' intelligence was a force to be reckoned with. It moved my respect for crows and their kindred to a different level.

I saw birds through others' eyes first. Many were friends: insect-eating robins, beautiful singing redbirds, weather-forecasting rain crows. Others were foes: crop-eating crows, death-dealing owls, pecan-stealing jays. The vast majority were neutral neighbors:

thrushes, warblers, vireos, tanagers, sparrows, buntings, and black-birds. I'm not sure anyone else noticed seasonal changes in their vast array.

At first the identities of the birds didn't really matter to me, either. The Home Place names were enough. There weren't differences between chipping sparrows or song sparrows; they were all just sparrows. I never knew that there were other red birds besides cardinals.

Then, one day, my matronly, gray-haired second-grade teacher, Mrs. Beasley, gave us mimeographed pictures of birds to color. The empty outline of that bird on the white page inspired me. I somehow knew the bird on the page was what Mamatha called a "markingbird"—a gray-and-white copycat songster that I saw and heard often on the Home Place—and so was given permission to pursue my ornithological obsession. Inside my seven-year-old psyche a switch was flipped on that would never be turned off. Not long after the mimeographed mockingbird's inspiration, I bought my first field guide—*A Golden Nature Guide to Birds.* The pocket-sized book was full of the birds I knew and many more I didn't. It gave some of the birds different names and stories that explained where they lived or even how they sounded. Soon my grandmother's birds became my ornithology. Her redbirds, bee-martins, yellowhammers, snowbirds, rain crows, partridges, buzzards, and chicken hawks became northern cardinals, eastern kingbirds, yellow-shafted flickers, slate-colored juncos, yellow-billed cuckoos, northern bobwhite, vultures, and red-tailed hawks. Perhaps I could still live some of my life's desires through birds. Even if I couldn't fly like them, I could watch them and imagine life on the wing.

I've watched hawks trace circles in the sky, connecting one circuit to another. I imagine they start these journeys by looking up. Then spiraling ever higher, until at some zenith the raptor's intuition tells it to break free and soar to the next point of rising.

How could I know that I, too, would one day find myself searching and circling? Several times a year I'm packed tightly into a metal-winged bird, plying the skies, zooming from one place to the next. There's relatively little fear of gravity taking over and the ground greeting me unceremoniously; I fly without a second thought, observing the landscape passing beneath me. Cross-country, east to west and back again, watching the irregular patchwork of farms and prairies meld with cities and suburbia. Much of it is sewn together by rivers. I see geometric precision, with center-pivot irrigation drawing circles of green in the parched land. I see amorphous patches of forest fragmented to islands where so many songbirds struggle. I cross bays and bayous. I travel from night into day and back again. I am finally flying. I wonder if there are any little brown boys earthbound beneath me, looking up.

Whose Eye Is on the Sparrow

There is special providence in the fall of a sparrow.

— William Shakespeare, *Hamlet*

Boys and BB guns—one existing without the other at some point before a boy earned his driver's license or hit drinking age was unknown growing up in the South. And so the Christmas morning when I finally found my answer to a whole year of praying, wishing, and not-so-subtle hints lying amidst all the other toys, I felt promoted to the next stage of boyhood. I was officially a *real* boy, transformed from a toy-playing, fake-wooden-gun-toting pretender. Like any good American male I was armed, ready to conquer and kill.

In the Lanham house Santa didn't bother wrapping the toys you'd requested. Instead he'd pack everything neatly in a box you left out for his convenience. And Santa had been especially generous that year: the BB gun was surrounded by a Lionel "Spirit of '76" train set, a couple of plastic model fighter planes, a folding pocketknife, a denim jacket, and a pile of candy, fruit, and nuts. I paid obligatory attention to most of the morning's other booty. But even as I marveled at the miniature exactness of the red, white, and blue diesel engine; imagined dogfights between the model airplanes; and fingered the shiny new knife blade in anticipation of using it to skin whatever big game I killed with my new rifle, my mind was firmly fixed on the Daisy Cub. I teased myself by saving the best for last. When I couldn't ignore the siren pleas any longer,

I tore into the cardboard case, not caring one bit about preserving the package, instructions, or set of targets on the back. I knew better, however, than to cock or aim the gun in the house. If Daddy saw me so much as play at shooting inside, I might not see the gun ever again. He insisted that we never, ever point a gun—even a play one—at anyone. A plastic pearl-handled cap revolver had already disappeared after I broke that Lanham law.

In hindsight the issue of gun safety in our house was not made much of. There were no gun safes or locked cabinets, and Daddy kept a small arsenal of rifles and shotguns stacked in the corner of the kitchen by the back-porch door. The ammunition was usually in a dresser drawer or on top of the freezer. The one pistol I ever saw, a rust-pitted silver revolver, stayed hidden in the tackle box. Daddy claimed it was for snakes; I assume he meant the slithering kind and not the two-legged variety. Mamatha's little single-shot .410 was always close by at her house, too. You had to be careful how you approached her door at night because she was quick to threaten a blast of birdshot if you hadn't called ahead.

In spite of the ready availability of enough firepower to arm a small nation, I can't remember the gun rules ever being broken. And so that Christmas morning, with the rules clear in my ten-year-old head, I had no intention of running afoul of any law that might separate me and the Cub. I caressed the cold blue metal barrel and traced my fingers over the words etched there: DAISY MFG. CO. ROGER, ARK. A notched sight and a blade, through which I would take dead aim at unwary quarry, interrupted the mostly smooth barrel. I tapped my knuckles against the shiny brown stock; I felt the ridges of the imitation wood grain and heard the satisfyingly hollow *whock* of injection-molded plastic. The gun was slicked with a coating of oil—the greasy aroma was intoxicating.

There I was, still safe in the comfort of the paneled den, and the little Daisy Cub was already my best friend. I knew that soon it would be a survival tool that would protect me in the great backyard and beyond. Sitting in the growing heap of garbage that Christmas mornings produce, I was already imagining distant targets falling to my yet-to-be-tested expert marksmanship. All those hours spent storming the Normandy beaches and hunting grizzly bears with rubber-band rifles and plastic pistols would finally pay off. Now at my disposal was the real deal.

There were plenty of rituals in the Lanham house beyond finding your box of stuff in the den on Christmas morning. The initial toy fest was always interrupted by breakfast. Afterward, Mama and Daddy would open their grown-up gifts. In my earliest years, we would all go out a couple of days before Christmas and find a worthy red cedar to grace the den. Pretty but prickly, the cedar filled the house with a sweet woodsy smell. Later on, though, Mama tired of the mess the tree made and bought an artificial one. It was the in-thing, and besides, it meant we could get the tree up earlier and with less work. The limbs were even color coded. At the end of construction the perfect spruce-pine-fir plastic tree stood in seven-foot-tall splendor. And although we sat around a fake tree, the joy was real. Ooohing and aaahing over everyone else's boring gifts, I couldn't wait to get out with my new gun. Who really cared about perfume and yarn crafting kits? Not me. But finally, with the formalities over, the Cub and I set out to tame the world—one brass BB at a time.

On that auspicious December day when the Daisy Cub and I came together I needed the proper expedition outfit. I shrugged on my hand-me-down coat, the one that looked like buckskin with a white fur collar. It was actually brown corduroy and fluffy cotton

pile, but from far away it looked just like the rugged gear the mountain men wore. I didn't have gloves or mittens, so I pulled a pair of
socks over my hands. The metal barrel full of brass BB shot sounded
like an angry rattler in my hands.

Outside I pulled the lever down and cocked the Cub. The rifle
came up easily to my shoulder and was lighter than I'd imagined it
would be. I rested my warm brown cheek on the cold brown stock
and drew a bead down the notched sight at a dangerous pine tree.
I pulled the trigger. The gentle nudge on my shoulder—what the
experts call recoil—was accompanied by the soft *ffft* of the little shot
leaving the barrel.

I could move my finger a fraction of an inch and send a projec-
tile into space with deadly intent! Holding perfect shooter's form
like that of all the cowboys and soldiers on television, I could actually see the shiny ball arc through the air and disappear into the
tree's corky bark. All those years of wishing and play had paid off;
I was a deadeye shot already. With the Home Place now safe from
menacing trees, I made my way around the yard, disabling armies
of tin cans, flocks of pinecones, and empty bottles full of imaginary
nitroglycerin that blew up in wishful explosions.

I was an expert now: a younger, browner reincarnation of
Daniel Boone, the Rifleman, John Wayne, and G. I. Joe, all rolled
into one. I was ready, I thought, for something more than pinecones, tin, and glass. I was ready to hunt something alive. Maybe I
could down a deer or turkey for that night's feast!

My hunting dreams faded fast. Even with my best stalking
techniques—stooping and stopping, creeping and crawling—every
living thing seemed to know that a new predator was out and about.
As I wandered through fallow fields of dead grass and corn stub-
ble, wary flocks of juncos flew just ahead of me. I imagined the

flocks were coveys of flushing quail or pheasants rising in a rush of feathers. I'd watched enough of *The American Sportsman* with Curt Gowdy on television to know that you had to swing through to hit the fast-flying targets. When they did it on the show a bird or two always fell. Trusty pointers and retrievers helped them find and fetch their targets. I had no dogs, but they wouldn't have helped me anyway. The twenty-yard range of my rifle and the physics of a single BB pushed by nothing more than a spring-loaded plunger and a blast of air did not make for effective hunting—I needed more cooperative quarry.

The yard wasn't wild like the fields and forests so I figured something less flighty might be found there. Besides I needed to get closer to the house so I could hear Mama's call for dinner. The long day of participating in the Battle of the Bulge, shooting buffalo bareback from a painted pony, and stalking quail, pheasants, cottontails, and deer had taken a lot out of me. I would need to replenish soon. But then, at the edge of the yard, I saw a different flock of birds hopping about. At my less-than-stealthy approach most flew away as quickly as the juncos in the field had done. But one little gray-and-brown bird flew only a short distance and perched tamely in a small pecan tree. I was close enough to see a small black pushpin eye that seemed not to have noticed me. I stalked closer, wanting desperately not to frighten the bird. It had a chestnut-colored cap and was about the same size as the birds I'd seen earlier. Oblivious, it sat there, rearranging misplaced feathers with a little cone-like beak. For a moment, I was mesmerized by the beauty of it. But in the next, I wanted only to point my gun at it and kill it.

All that I saw—the bird's beauty, its tameness, its innocence— didn't matter to me that morning. I was on a single-minded

mission to make something die with my new power and no sen-
timentality entered into the very simple equation. I lined up the
sparrow's clean, gray breast in my sights, pushed the plastic safety
forward to fire, and pulled the trigger. Like every shot before, the
stock nudged my shoulder, the plunger pushed the column of air
through the tube, and the minute brassy ball raced through the
chill air. But this time, it flew not into unfeeling bark or tough,
unloving metal. This time, I watched at first in satisfaction but
then in horror as the BB traced its path to the place where I'd
aimed. In all of my practice that day, I had accurately accounted
for the arcing distance the ball had to travel. Drop compensation
had become a part of every shot I made. My eyeball physics paid
off this time. The shot flew true, straight into the end of the little
bird's life. The abrupt whisper of the gun was followed almost
immediately by a sound I had not heard before. Not a satisfying
plink into tin, or a crackling tinkle of broken glass, but a sudden
and sickening *thwack*, as the BB found its mark in the breast of
the sparrow.

The bird didn't try to fly away. It didn't even flutter. It just fell—
awkwardly—from its perch and hit the ground, flopping pitifully
for what seemed like a long time. And then it was still. I walked
the few steps to where it lay and looked at what I had done. The
bird wasn't stunned or injured. It was dead. I was suddenly terrified and surprised at the same time. I had done what I had set
out to do and killed something, but when I stared at the dead bird
lying on the ground, I was ashamed of the deed, afraid to even pick
the lifeless form up. It was a chipping sparrow, brown cap, black
eye stripe, and gray breasted, just like the one I'd seen in some
of my bird books. It was as close as the pictures on the pages—
and dead. With all my earlier brazenness to take another life, now

I stood alone with my conscience—and the sparrow—trembling and regretting what I had done.

Had I intended to eat the sparrow maybe I could've made sense of my actions. But no, I had simply gone out to kill, to see something die as a direct result of a decision I'd made. I tried to figure out how I would hide what felt like a crime. I looked around to see who—or what—was watching and prayed for forgiveness as I finally gathered the courage to pick up the limp sparrow. It was still warm. There was no blood, but its wings hung limply and the life in its once bright eyes was gone.

I buried the bird at the edge of the yard, in a hastily scraped, shallow grave not too far from the pecan tree. I thought I was hiding the deed from everyone and everything. I'd been out there for hours without doing harm to more than cans and cones. But suddenly there was damage—deadly damage. Mama called for dinner, but I'd lost my appetite. I placed the gun in the corner. The Daisy Cub was no longer a toy. It belonged with the other lethal weapons.

Daddy's warning about pointing guns at things fell hard on me that day. I still used the little gun but it never killed again. I left that Christmas behind with my feelings for feathered creatures—and life—forever changed.

Cows

A cow is as good as a man.

⌁ Masai proverb

WHEN DADDY USED TO PLAY THE SONS OF THE PIONEERS SINGING "Tumbling Tumbleweeds" and "Riders in the Sky," the wavering harmonies floated through the Ranch like prairie ghosts. From the halls, images of wide-open spaces, happy days in the saddle, and sunsets painting the desert seeped into my consciousness. For as long as I can remember I've wanted to be a cowboy: a spur-jinglin', chaps-a-flappin', ten-gallon-hat-wearin', lasso-throwin', painted-horse-ridin', six-gun-totin' cowboy. I saw no problem fitting that in with my other careers as fighter pilot and ornithologist. I would be the world's first bird-watching, calf-roping, sonic-booming black man.

The fantasy of the horse-riding Westerner was further burned into my growing brain by the scorching brand of Hollywood and Technicolor. Built into the appeal of being under big sky on the back of a sturdy steed was the idea of having John Wayne's swagger, Clint Eastwood's cool, and Marshal Matt Dillon's resolve for right. The excitement and danger of a long cattle drive from deep in the heart of Texas to somewhere wilder and even wool-lier, like Colorado or Montana, glimmered enticingly. In the set of Compton's Encyclopedias that I consulted on an almost daily basis, my favorite volumes were *B* for birds; *C* for cattle, Colorado, and cowboys; and *M* for Montana.

It was a largely white world that I grew up in. My schoolmates were mostly white. My best friends were white. The westerns I watched were homogenized, too: milky, alabaster, ivory. Besides the occasional Mexican bandit, the horses were the only beings of color. Roscoe Lee Browne's role as Jebediah Nightlinger, the surly but brave and occasionally poetic chuck wagon cook in the John Wayne movie *The Cowboys*, was the singular suggestion that black people ever ventured beyond the Mississippi River. It wasn't until I was well into my teen years that I learned there had been black men who were in fact vital cogs of Western culture. I was heartened to know there had been people who shared my color bronco busting, roping, riding herd, and doing all the things I saw as defining the West. Some historians claim that up to a third of the cowboys on many of the great cattle-drive trails were black men—slaves and former slaves who found a degree of freedom and respect on the prairies and high plains. The names that should be famous—Nat "Deadwood Dick" Love, Bill Pickett, Bose Ikard, "Stagecoach" Mary Fields—are seldom sung by the cowboy balladeers.

If I'd paused on my frequent journeys to Montana in Compton's *M* volume, I might have even seen the tall, proud Masai warriors clothed in red robes and roaming the East African plains behind herds of massively horned cattle. These people looked more like me and were more intimately connected to cattle than any boot-wearing white man. The sky above the Mara reserve rivals anything we might imagine in the American West. The bushman's golden grass waves under the bellies of wildebeests, elephants, and zebras instead of bison, pronghorn, and mule deer. The Masai don't ride horses but they're tough, living among lions and leopards with only spears and knives to defend themselves. But like the Tuskegee Airmen—or the idea that anyone looking like me could watch birds—black cowboys in general were absent from the cultural conversation of the 1970s. All of the things that I wanted to be or do seemed colorless. It was discouraging.

I never killed a lion with my bare hands, or drank the blood flowing fresh and hot from the neck of a living cow, rode drag on a painted pony, or sang a herd of ornery longhorns to sleep under a starry western sky. Still my connection to the bovine kind runs thick. I grew up with cows that we thought enough of to give names: Brooksy, Ol' Mary, Nelly-Bell, Blackie, and Bill the Bull. Cows were a constant fixture on the Home Place and much of our lives revolved around getting them fed, turning them out, putting them up, cursing them, castrating them, losing them, finding them, hauling them, selling them, killing them, and ultimately eating them. So many cattle-centered activities that in retrospect I suppose the cows with names—and even those without—were almost family, four-legged, cloven-hoofed, sloe-eyed, ruminating, farting family.

The Home Place year was defined by falling leaves, gobbling toms, muggy thunderstorms, and frost-covered fields. It was defined by time spent shocking drying corn into golden teepees, finding a wobbly legged calf in greening spring pastures, the never-ending fence mending, and feeding up the herd in the early dark of a cold November night. For all of the work that it takes to keep cows, there is *always* more. Unlike in the westerns I used to watch, there were no cow ponies. The cattle drives were never long and dusty. There was never any branding or roping or river crossing of a thousand head of lowing beeves. The work was not nearly so romantic or so dangerous—but it was constant.

The work that often got us out of bed—or sometimes kept us from it—was simply a part of the Home Place routine. More than any other labor—more than cutting and hauling firewood, mowing the grass, or feeding the hogs—tending the cows was the domino that set every other action in motion and the monkey wrench that could grind it to a halt. Cows didn't celebrate Christmas, Easter, or the Fourth of July. They never took vacation. And so day after day, for all of my time on the Home Place, the cows took precedence. What did they give in return? Meat, of course. We had a steer or two slaughtered every year. The finely marbled muscle fed us and much of our extended family, too.

To achieve this end product, the herd of twenty to forty animals consumed enormous amounts of biomass: sweet feed, cow candy consisting of wheat, oats, and corn tinted with sticky molasses; Bermuda hay, ripened and dried in the summer swelter; and of course pasturage, acres and acres of grass. Daddy rotated the herd between this pasture and that to let the forage recover. Usually the Bermuda and fescue grass that made the hay was cheap and plentiful. Sweet feed—and the armada of tractors, harrows, disks, bailers, harvesters, trucks, and manpower necessary to process it—was not. The cows grew fat and sleek on what we raised on the Home Place and the hay from friendly farmer neighbors. Moneywise they were at best a break-even proposition. Mama would say years later that sometimes the cows ate at our expense. She and Daddy occasionally argued about whether to buy hay for cows or groceries for us.

The cows were often stress-inducing machines, too. There was never enough hay or feed; there was always a fence down somewhere; the sweat equity put in was never cashed out. Unless you're subsidized to raise your beef on public land at pennies on the dollar, you're destined to always owe more than you make. But Daddy kept the cows, sold a few, bought a few—almost always for little or no financial gain. The few pennies earned were usually plowed back into the herd.

It was a love-hate proposition for Daddy. I think he hated the business of it—the dollars and cents—but he loved seeing things grow and thrive. From raising up the pasturage that the cows ate to seeing the new calves galloping about to providing several families with enough protein to last for a year, there was a cycle to it all and he was the wheelmaster.

His passion rubbed off on me. There was never much said about the work I did. Daddy just expected the feeding and fence mending to get done. But I liked the responsibility so much that on a couple of occasions I proudly wore my brogan work shoes to school, reeking of the smelly stuff the cows left behind. My "sophisticated" suburban classmates laughed and made fun of me but my father noticed the dedication.

One day Daddy loaded onto the truck a fat "black baldy" steer, the product of a Hereford cow and a Black Angus bull. I hopped into the truck alongside him for the silent ride to the slaughter-house. Occasionally the truck would shift slightly as the heavy animal moved to and fro. Even though I spent a great deal of time with the cows we fattened up for the dinner table, I didn't get attached. Those animals never had names. We drove toward Saluda, where the nameless animals were always off-loaded on four feet and picked up a week later wrapped in wax paper. The steer bawled. Daddy always said that the cows could smell the death coming. But then instead of turning toward the slaughterhouse, Daddy drove on. We kept going through town until we arrived at the stockyard.

A smelly city of corrals populated by cattle and a few horses, goats, and sheep, the stockyard was a fascinating place. I looked forward to visiting the maze of pens, chutes, and runs as much as other kids might look forward to going to a candy store. I could spend hours on the catwalk, watching the handlers move animals here and there. Eventually all of these animals would end up in the auction room, where a big scale registered their weight and a man spoke faster than I could understand. As he rattled off numbers people nodded and wiggled fingers that apparently meant "I want to buy that cow." So there we were, Daddy, the black baldy, and me.

I had guessed at this point that we were going to sell the steer to someone else instead of eating it. When our steer's turn at auction came, there was a small buzz. The scale wound around to almost eight hundred pounds and more men waved and wiggled their fingers than usual. While most animals spent less than half a minute on the scale our cow was there much longer. Finally someone waved or wiggled the right way and the auctioneer said, "Sold!" The white-faced steer got a prod in its fat rump and cantered off the stage. Daddy seemed pleased. When he picked up the $713 check at the auction office, he signed it over to me. That sudden windfall was like hitting the lottery. That was Daddy's gift, my reward for my dedication to the cows, but what was *his* reward? What benefit did he reap from all the hours of hard work?

Daddy occasionally spoke of selling off the herd, but it never happened. The cows were so much more than stress and labor to Daddy. They were a release from things that he could not control, four-legged confessors. He loved those cows.

I saw that one afternoon as he was sitting on the front porch watching the herd grazing. Heads down, a dozen or so Black Angus heifers and steers, Nelly-Bell, a couple of her black baldy calves, and Bill the Bull were all oriented as if some bovine magnet had drawn them in the same direction. Over the whining of the katydids you could hear the rhythmic shearing of grass as the cows mowed their way across the sun-dappled slope. The tall pines scattered here and there cast long shadows through the group. Daddy's gaze held the view but went somewhere beyond it. It was as fine a summer day as ever was and all the herd were accounted for. The fences were mended, the hay was growing thick in the fields, and the worry of winter feeding was months away yet. The cows were contented. Daddy was, too.

~

I travel west now and my youthful fantasies are reborn when I take in the sweep of mountain ranges and grasslands under end-less canopies of blue sky. What I see on a Colorado Front Range prairie or in the Montana Bitterroot Valley stirs the same feelings that my sojourns through the encyclopedias did. I've stood on the banks of the Rio Grande and imagined herds of lanky longhorn cattle and feisty mustangs crossing the muddy swales. The rolling Nebraska Sandhills and dancing prairie chickens; the sky islands of the Arizona Chiricahuas and croaking, elegant trogons; the cold-running streams of Yosemite and diving American dippers; the buttes of Montana and soaring golden eagles; the Texas Big Bend and skulking Colima warbler; the Kansas tallgrass and sing-ing dickcissels—it's a bucket list of Western places and species for American birders. Like most of the places I go to see birds any-where in the world, these spots are often far off the beaten path and mostly populated by white people. As I seek rare birds, I often find myself among the rarest individuals around.

I can take pride, however, in knowing I'm not the first black man to set foot on this arid soil. So many of the far-flung, bird-rich locations I travel to grabbed the attention of black soldiers first. The famed Buffalo Soldiers of the US Army's 9th and 10th Cavalry units and 24th and 25th Infantry units were there over a hundred years before me. They were sent to the far ends of the frontier to hold the line and press the manifest destiny of a growing nation, and endured the extremes of heat, cold, dust, mud, insects, and disease. But I like to think there were quiet times among the daily tasks of surviving racism, skirmishes with ill-treated American Indians, and incursions from Mexican desperados. Maybe on an evening watch, a black man in a blue woolen waistcoat looked skyward, his ears catching the trumpeting calls of thousands of sandhill cranes setting their wings against the falling sun. Perhaps the symphony soothed some of the angry edge sharpened by poor pay and even less respect. Perhaps a brown-faced horseman, the son of a slave, with knee boots dusty from the trail and a broad-brimmed hat slouched low over tired eyes, wondered aloud at the spectacle of a snipe twittering to the heavens one minute and spiraling to the ground the next.

A two-lined phalanx of black men on bay mounts must have been impressive as they wound their way across rolling grassland, the eerie cries of long-billed curlews and the sweet songs of western meadowlarks melding with the sounds of creaking saddle leather and jingling bridle rings. A bold pair of acrobatic, scissor-tailed flycatchers takes advantage of the flying feast kicked up by the horses' hooves and a trooper marvels at the grace of the birds as they swoop in and out of the column.

The West has always seemed an open canvas to me. Perhaps the same thing that draws me there now drew those brave men back then. The black soldiers who found themselves out west lived hard but free lives. Though my dreams of being a cowboy died long ago, my love for places defined by mountain ranges that reach the clouds and plains expanses that claim the horizon lives on.

Life's Spring

High technology has done us one great service: It has retaught us the delight of performing simple and primordial tasks—chopping wood, building a fire, drawing water from a spring.

—— Edward Abbey,
A Voice Crying in the Wilderness

WATER CLEANS. IT PURIFIES. IT IS THE SUBSTANCE FROM WHICH life itself crawled to become *us*. Edgefield's creeks—Stevens, Turkey, Cheves, Horns, Shaw's, Dry Branch; some ruddy and rocky, others sandy and foamy—are at this very moment tumbling and flowing to feed the mighty Savannah River and the Atlantic Ocean beyond. In some places the perpetual motion slacks in backwaters, swamps, sloughs, and beaver marsh. In others the flow is stemmed by humans playing God, creating lakes that bring cheap electricity and recreation to the millions downstream demanding both. From clouds and rainfall to streams and creeks, lakes and ponds, the sea, and back again to the heavens, water is the lifeblood of us all.

As enticing as creeks can be, as inspiring as lake sunsets are, water more humbly born is where it all begins. In seeps and quiet oozing, this water works its way upward and outward from unseen aquifers. Deep beneath the piedmont's crust it flows like a circulatory system.

We grew up drinking springwater that was sweet, cool, and

nothing like the tainted stuff that spurted obscenely on push-button command from school fountains. There was something in that water, filtered through treatment facilities and made safe by a cocktail of chemicals, that just didn't taste right. Our water at the Home Place came from a perpetually dark and dank little bottom just a buck's bound or two down the hill from Mamatha's house. Its first and most efficient filter was clay, loam, and leaves. The soil and litter leached in natural chemicals. The network was simple, built on leak-prone, black PVC pipe. The water moved at the urging of moody, underpowered electric pumps. There was a great deal of hope in the system, too. Hope that the occasional deep freezes wouldn't be deep enough (or long enough) to stop the flow. Hope that the thaw wouldn't reveal leaks. Hope that droughts wouldn't drain the supply. Hope that the pumps would function reliably. Hope that the sweet water would always be there.

Barring his inability to control drought and hard freezes, Daddy was the god we all put our faith in to keep that water flowing. On the rare occasions when it didn't, our water had to come from another source. Cheves Creek then became more than our favorite fishing hole. It was temporary life support. We filled fifty-five-gallon barrels from the fishy-smelling creek and used their contents to irrigate the garden, water the hogs, and flush the toilets. Once boiled, we cooked meals and washed the dishes and ourselves with the water. Eventually the dry times slacked or the ice thawed, and Daddy kept the system going.

The spring was the mechanical heart of the Home Place. Like the beating of our own hearts, which we often take for granted, life without that water was hard to envision. Day after day we expected that the pumping would sustain us. Even when the flow stopped for a day or a week, we knew that Daddy would resuscitate the erratic organ and bring it back into time, and that the flow would resume its rhythm.

But we are given only so many lub-dubbing cycles by the muscular machine that beats in our chests. It will inevitably fail us all. Heroic efforts and technology only temporarily prolong what none of us can escape. I know now that the water flowing from the spring was the clear and sparkling lifeblood of the Home Place, the man-made pump-heart pushing sustenance throughout the network of plastic pipe arteries to the organs that depended on it. So when Daddy's heart stopped beating one day, I think we all knew deep down that it wouldn't be long before life changed on the Home Place in many other ways.

There's a picture of my father taken a couple of years before he died. In it he appears much older than forty-nine or fifty. His eyes are deep set and tired, and seem to see something beyond his surroundings. His hair is much grayer than it had been just a year or two before. There's a tension in his jaw that I can feel through the photo paper. The picture shows my father dying. Something inside him was changing—something unwatered, withering. There was too much stress from too many worries over things he couldn't control. I think it was a leak in his soul's cistern that only he knew existed. In the end it drained his life away.

Daddy died in April, the season of gentle rains that would recharge the aquifers that fed the Home Place spring. He died just as the plum trees and apple orchard exploded with blossoms. He died as the longbeards gobbled for love in the bottom and new calves were born. He died as our relationship was evolving into something more than it had been.

Daddy died of stubbornness and toughness as much as from a heart attack. He never did anything for his ongoing chest troubles beyond obtaining nitroglycerin pills for the pain. Daddy's way was to endure. Pain was simply an inconvenience, one he hardly ever acknowledged. Sickness was something that happened to others. I don't remember a time when my father wasn't doing something toward making life better on the Home Place. It was who he was— never relenting, never giving in. This firmness served him well in many ways and at many times: his persistence kept things going, kept the spring flowing. He heroically freed the obstructions that sometimes kept the water from getting to us, but he could not free himself of the strains that eventually stopped the lifeblood from flowing through his heart.

Daddy's death meant that the spring would die, too. It began a season of change. Soon after he left, our inability to keep the Home Place's heart pumping and arteries clear made the decision easy. We couldn't live without water, so Mama hired a well puncher who drilled a two-hundred-foot hole through the clay and rock until water erupted from the dirty puncture in the ground. The hum of the new heart was smooth and unerring but the water it pumped was never as sweet.

Sometimes I dream of the spring still gurgling and flowing. The brick-red cistern was a mystical place to me. On occasion I'd sneak down to the little bottom and lift the lid on the cistern to see if a brilliant red salamander was hiding there. But I haven't visited the bottom since Daddy died. It's surely overgrown now.

The salamanders have the choked cistern and the seep to themselves. Wild turkeys and whitetails might find a cool puddle here and there to slake their summer thirsts. Maybe barking foxes still welcome misty mornings from the depths of the damp hollow. I would imagine that the copperheads retook their spring-bottom kingdom and guard it jealously. I wouldn't venture to challenge them for it. Water is life and often a resurrective force. What grows and dwells there now is maybe what is supposed to be.

～

Water on the Home Place drives a certain longing. Fishing was the only time I remember ever holding my father's hand. There was a ford we had to cross to reach the foam-covered fishing hole at Cheves Creek, where the family often wet a line on summer after-noons. The ford was often snot-slick with slime. Upstream of the crossing, the creek surged slow and brown like sorghum syrup. As it approached the ford it picked up speed, pouring noisily over and down into the fishing hole. The ford's footing was unsure at best and crossing it unaided was dangerous.

Daddy's big calloused hand swallowed mine, his thick fingers like steel bands. I knew I was safe in that grasp. My faith in it was complete. Though such purposeful physical contact was a rare thing between us, these moments were enough to etch something deep. I've seldom had that kind of abiding faith in anyone or anything since.

The rushing creek water crooned a lullaby. The river music interlaced with birdsong and the insects droning in the humid-ity of a July evening made summer a special time. Fishing was one of Daddy's escapes. It was how he played, and how he fed us, too, sometimes. The fishing-hole forays almost always involved the family, and it never seemed to me that we went often enough. Sometimes Daddy went on longer fishing expeditions to the big water—Clarks Hill—the hydroelectric lake a few miles north of the Home Place. Those were usually solitary trips but on some of them one of his close friends would go along. They'd often return with few, if any, fish. On a couple of occasions, Daddy and I would head off by ourselves to Lick Fork, a small lake where I learned to swim alongside catfish, bream, and few large-mouthed bass that patrolled the murky water. On these occasions there were never many words. But there didn't have to be. It was solid time, deep time. I felt worthy just being in Daddy's presence. It didn't matter whether the fish bit or not.

On a good day at the fishing hole, the bobbers would hit the water and within a minute or two there would be a twitch, then another. If the thing underwater was worth its weight in cornmeal and hot grease, the bobber would disappear like a torpedo into the depths, taking a foot or two of stiffening line with it. On the other end, I could feel the strength of whatever it was that had sucked in the unlucky worm. Pulled back, but not too hard, the cane pole curved with the catch. The line would cut and dance in the water for a few seconds as the slab of muscle struggling to stay under flashed like quicksilver. The fights never lasted very long. With a tug and more than a few whoops and hollers, a hand-sized blue-gill or maybe a brilliant redbreast hung flipping and wriggling on the other end of the line.

For a few years after James Hoover Lanham died, I would occasionally dream about him. These dreams, too, were filled with water. The last time I went fishing with Daddy, he'd already been dead for a couple of years; for a while fishing was how I connected with him in the afterlife. In those dreams I could never see his face. We would sit in the boat, me astern and him in the bow, both casting our lines out into the vastness of a dreamscape. Time after time we'd cast and reel, cast and reel—but there were never any fish. I always seemed on the verge of saying something that needed to be said. I suppose Daddy kept coming back through that subconscious portal to give me another opportunity to speak. The night he finally turned around to face me, however, he didn't say a word. I've not seen him again in the watery dream realm.

The last day I saw Daddy alive wasn't extraordinary in any way. He dropped Mama and me off at Schofield High. For maybe a year or two at that point, I'd made a habit of telling Daddy to have a good day as we left the car. It was a part of that growing relationship between us. That spring day, I reached out to shake my father's hand in what was to be the final contact we would ever have. There was no water between us then, but the warmth of lifeblood that flowed from skin to skin, a warmth that still sustains me.

There's water always cycling around us. Sometimes it comes in a spring's quiet seep, sustaining life in imperceptible flow. Sometimes it comes in a storm's raging deluge, sweeping away the familiar to force new beginnings. For years after the storm of Daddy's death, I thought about water. I dreamed about water. Odd, though, was the absence of water where it should have been. There was very little crying in my family when Daddy died, though I heard Mama sobbing in her bedroom one night. I can't remember more than a drizzling of tears from the rest of us. That was just our family; growing up, I'd mostly associated tears with physical pain.

And so I didn't fully, deeply mourn the death of my father for almost thirty years. Through all of that time without him—college, growing up with my own family, career building, the ups and downs of life—there was no time for remembering what had been. I finally broke down when I was in my forties. An assignment from a writing-workshop instructor to compose a five-hundred-word essay on "place" for the next day's class unlocked the floodgates. I fretted over what to write through most of the evening. Late that night, in a spartan dorm room in Craftsbury Common, Vermont,

I began to craft a piece about my boyhood memories of family and the Home Place. I struggled at first, not sure which way the river of words would bend. But once the words began to flow I couldn't stop them. Almost two thousand words beyond the assigned count I put the essay away. The next morning I tried to read the words I'd written to five women I didn't know in a place I'd spent hardly any time. Many of them had already let their tears flow freely over the words they'd shared—about memories of love for people and places, and of painful losses, too. They'd unwittingly given me permission to be someone I'd never been. As I waded through the words of what my life with Daddy had been, the dam broke. Some spring deep within me welled up. I cried, and the water that was my life cycled through me.

I seem to have since crossed a bridge. It's not uncommon for me to cry now. Sorrow and pain—losses of loved ones—bring tears out in slow ebbs. But they also come in the happiest moments. A full moon rising to make the forest glow in cold fire, a winter sunset burnishing a bay salt marsh in every imaginable hue, or a thrush singing sweetly from within a dark wood are all just cause for letting the water flow freely.

Flight

The Bluebird of Enlightenment

A man's interest in a single bluebird is worth more than
a complete but dry list of the fauna and flora of a town.

⌐ Henry David Thoreau

IT WAS THE FOURTH OF JULY AND INSTEAD OF SWEATING NEAR
a barbecue or swilling a beer, I was working. I had the bird in
my scope and was reading the plastic color bands on its leg. Left:
mauve over green; right: mauve over silver. It was the same male
usually found at this box. I sighed. Nothing new to report here. It
was just another day of trying to understand bluebird sex.

My job for the summer was checking eastern bluebird nest
boxes and weighing, measuring, banding, and bleeding the little
pinfeathered chicks to see if the brilliant blue male that typically attended each box was indeed the little one's DNA daddy.
But these bluebirds weren't exactly symbols of happiness for me.
After the first few blissful, bird-filled weeks of fieldwork, the routine had gotten old—old, tiring, and hot. It was a typical South
Carolina July—hotter than hell and humid enough for gills. For
six days out of every week since March I'd puttered around in my
little fading-from-silver-to-gray, unair-conditioned 1981 Honda
Civic. It was my field vehicle—transportation and banding lab
in one.

My subject, the eastern bluebird or *Sialia sialis*, was the familiar blue thrush, with a burnished chest and belly, that finds its
place along fencerows, pastures, and open meadows. A conservation

success story, eastern bluebirds went from being threatened with extinction in the early to mid-twentieth century to being a common backyard bird that people readily claim as their own. They live in human-hewn nest boxes instead of competing for the scarce natural cavities that so many other birds covet. People everywhere are enchanted with the birds' beauty, soothing songs, and apparently gentle natures. But these attributes lead to certain assumptions about lifestyle. Monogamous, heterosexual, married. My job was to help prove or disprove these thoughts about utter avian happiness.

The study was essentially a test of the long-held belief that birds, especially attractive passerines like eastern bluebirds, are faithful to one another for life. Anything else was unthinkable for a harbinger of happiness and fair weather.

Unthinkable, and yet Dr. Patricia Adair Gowaty thought it. While birds do it and bees do it, she argued, they don't do it like we think they do. She practiced good science with a keen feminist edge. She knew that research doesn't exist in a vacuum, and sought to present evidence for extending the argument beyond the birds. Politics, ornithology, and human sexual behavior were all on the daily menu. For weeks, I'd been on this research project, faithfully gathering some of the data that would soon make Patty famous in our field. Despite my exhaustion, being part of an elite National Science Foundation research team headed by the brilliant avian ecologist was an honor. Patty was pushing the limits of what we knew about bird sexual behavior. Her research assistants were intense and supercompetent mentors who had already taught me a great deal about field ornithology and how science was to be done. I was lucky. This was my first real exposure to my newly minted zoology major.

A good showing on this project would put me on the fast track to graduate school and becoming a bird-brained scientist at last.

⌒

Just a few months before, however, I'd been wallowing in a morass of indecision. I'd gone to Clemson University as a mechanical engineering major because I was a black kid who was reasonably good at math and science. That could only mean one or two things, according to the high school career counselors: become an engineer or a physician. And so that's where many of us ended up. The counselors suggested that, after all, engineering would help me earn the lifestyle to enjoy birds as a hobby.

And so I followed the edicts of those who were supposed to know better. I was the good soldier, the A-student who never rebelled. But all of that obedience came with a price. My happiness waned. After several summers of excruciatingly boring internships reading safety manuals and serving as a glorified gopher for equally boring engineers, I grew to hate engineering and anything associated with it. On my way to and from some dull class about mechanical stress and strain exerted on blocks, ropes, and pulleys, I'd feel pulled toward Long Hall, the biological-sciences building. People were inside doing what I really wanted to do.

After three years of suffering through what others had planned for me I wrestled my own fate to the ground, in what is perhaps the most courageous act I've ever performed. It was my junior year. I wasn't doing badly as an engineering student, grade-wise. I was also popular, a frat boy with a pretty girlfriend. On the outside life was almost perfect. But I was rotting on the inside. On that spring day, I stopped in my tracks on the way to the last engineering class I would ever attend and reversed the course of my destiny. I lost my full-ride DuPont scholarship and found my life.

⁓

Now here I was, far away from moments of inertia and rates of deceleration, out under the biggest, bluest sky, surrounded by singing birds in fields and forests that stretched as far as the eye could see. I'd always dreamed of this kind of life. But today, July 4, 1985— in the heat and stillness—I simply wanted a day away from these damned birds.

Day after day, I'd worked from dawn until the tasks were done, checking the wooden nest boxes that sat chest high on hundreds of fence posts. Once the neatly built nests of dead grass or pine straw had appeared in early spring, it had only been a day or two until the first sky-blue egg appeared. From that point on, the boxes were monitored closely and constantly to understand who was tending home. Was the same female always incubating? Was the same male always in the vicinity of the box? Were there interlopers of either sex? A high-powered spotting scope and the uniquely colored leg bands on each bird would tell part of the story.

For most of the boxes, a pair of bluebirds would uneventfully build a nest, incubate, and raise a brood of four to six little ones. The scene through the scope soon became boring. The bucolic landscape outside the lens, which once felt profoundly peaceful, became boring as well. But sometimes the peace of the pastoral was broken. There were some rather unfriendly encounters among the bluebirds, feather-flinging fights between both males and females in which a well-placed beak might kill the other bird.

Roughly two weeks from the appearance of the first egg, the pink, thimble-sized chicks appeared. Though fragile, blind, and seemingly mindless, the tiny lumps of flesh instinctively responded to the box lid being lifted, their lemon-yellow-lined mouths yawning wide for food that I didn't have. In a few days, I would return to find their eyes opened and pinfeathers erupted to reveal whether they were males or females. At that point, I became a bluebird nestling's nightmare, appearing without warning to poke, prod, and bleed, gathering DNA evidence. Most of the time, the adults simply waved their wings and warbled soft protests from a nearby perch. At a couple of boxes, though, the putative parents were more protective, dive-bombing me from the surrounding pines.

On easy days there were just ten or twenty boxes to check and I'd be done before noon. On this day, however, there seemed to be hundreds of things to do. Somehow all of the bluebirds on the route had conspired against me and decided to start new nests, lay eggs, hatch, fledge, or otherwise ruin my plans for having just a bit of the Fourth of July for myself.

In spite of the intense heat, the long work hours, a car that felt like an oven, and a bad attitude, I finally got through the day. And though the romanticized ideal of fieldwork was fading into the reality of disciplined routine, there were birds beyond the blue ones that helped me understand just how lucky I was. A green wheat field full of black-and-buff bobolinks singing like discordant music boxes and bandit-masked loggerhead shrikes impaling their prey on barbed wire fences broke the monotony into palatable bites. In cattle pastures, eastern meadowlarks whistled their sweet "spring-o'-the-year" songs, and one day a scissor-tailed flycatcher flung far from its midwestern moorings made a brief appearance on a fence line. And I'll never forget the upland sandpiper that perched atop a fencepost with its wings lifted in the midmorning sun, "back from Argentina," just as if Aldo Leopold had scripted the scene himself.

That summer proved to be the genesis of my ornithological career. After I proved myself with Patty, Dr. Sidney Gauthreaux, a pioneer of radar ornithology, took me on as a graduate student. His mentoring pushed me to become a better field scientist.

And the bluebirds? What did we learn? There was enough sex and violence in their world to put soap operas and trashy talk show television to shame. The voyeurism and lab work showed that not only was paternity uncertain, with males floating around to find sex everywhere, but females were much more in control of who was "lovin'" whom than anyone had previously believed. Some females were also involved in complex behaviors, like dumping their eggs in other females' nests. It was a passerine free-for-all out there. Patty had her data. Her research-backed insistence that females were as fully capable of actions popularly reserved for males—like freely seeking sex and controlling their own genetic fates—were foundational for changing the minds of those thinking about animal behavior and defining our thoughts about human behavior with more plasticity as well.

That day and all the others on the bluebird project were worth the minor sacrifices I made. There would be other holidays to squander. Patty gave me the chance to do fabulous science, and I learned that uncertainty was more the rule than the exception in nature. I find myself now trying to do what Patty did, falling into questions of what, why, and how not just in relation to how our wild kindred thrive but how we do, too.

Most of my life has been ruled by convention, an attachment to certainty, and trying to meet everyone else's expectations. The rules set down by society, my parents, Mamatha, and even God were supposed to be the guaranteed recipe for success: Do as you're told. Follow the prescribed path and you'll go far. Although my mind had been stretched by a few experiences earlier in college—noncommittal sex, a little experimentation with some mind-bending chemicals, and a hard political lean to the left—before my summer with the bluebirds the clearest path was still the narrow one. My upbringing taught me certain things about sex: never do it by yourself; never do it outside of marriage; always do it with a female; and always, always, always remember, God is watching wherever or whenever you do it. That was a scary thought—God watching me do it like I watched the bluebirds. But either God cared less about how bluebirds screwed around, or there was something more to sex than I'd been told about.

Black and white, good and evil—ideas harped on by religious folks, preached from some pulpit, or broadcast on television—were an ice on the pool of my consciousness. There are preconceived notions—of where I should go, of what I should do, and even of who I should do it with—of who I am supposed to be as a black man. But my choice of career and my passion for wildness means that I will forever be the odd bird, the raven in a horde of white doves, the blackbird in a flock of snow buntings.

In nature the only absolute truths are life and death, eat or die, pass your genes on into the future or disappear from the evolutionary landscape. Sex and hunger drive survival. It is that simple. As I listen to a wood thrush throw its song into a half-lit forest or watch a rutted-up buck circle downwind to catch the scent of a hot doe, I understand that I'm watching a straightforward struggle to exist and make more. I take comfort in the directness. There is no evil in nature.

The years have melted, softened, much that I once saw as black and white, morphing it into shades of gray. My good is Aldo Leopold's good: an ethic of inclusion, promoting the wholeness of nature and treating the land and the wild things that live on it as fellow citizens to be respected and nurtured. As Leopold wrote, "Harmony with land is like harmony with a friend; you cannot cherish his right hand and chop off his left." In driving creatures to extinction and decimating habitats without so much as a backward glance or lingering regret, human hands create disharmony. That, to me, is evil.

We humans put ourselves on a pedestal. The imperative is the same, though: survive, eat, and reproduce. Throw in emotion and things get complicated. We judge and stereotype and hate and love. I'll never be completely wild, never truly leave the domesticated world where expectations and feelings rule.

But I try to live half-wild, not judging, skirting convention and expectation. I spent too many years inside four walls. I have little blue thrushes to thank for my release.

Hoops

I'm a sworn enemy of convention. I despise the conventional in anything.

⟶ Hedy Lamarr

IN SPITE OF MY RELIGIOUS QUESTIONING AND SPRINT AWAY FROM fundamentalism, much of my life has been orthodox—and successful, by almost anyone's measure, because of it. I've never failed a grade, been arrested, fathered illegitimate children, or even had a negative wisp of gossip curl back around to me. Outside of a first-grade transgression, when I sketched an anatomically correct nude woman and my parents bargained with the principal not to expel me from school, I was Mamatha's and Daddy's favored child and frequently the teacher's pet. I was a Boy Scout, too, earning merit badges, living by the oaths and pledges, achieving my Life rank but falling just short of Eagle when my troop disintegrated. I was a mostly A student from kindergarten through high school, and a student body president in junior and senior high.

I never broke my mother's curfew and the few girls I dated before college didn't have anything to fear from me other than wandering hands. I was afraid of going further with them—the voices of guilt, shame, and sin planted firmly in my head by all the years of Baptist brainwashing warned me constantly that my life would be ruined by an accidental pregnancy. The fun, the voices said, wasn't worth the risk. And so despite backseat forays on dark back roads, I remained a virgin until I was nineteen.

Though my life has been sweet and rewarding in many ways, I'll be the first to admit I've stayed between the lines. I'm the consummate hoops jumper. I remember walking across the Clemson commencement stage, shaking the university president's hand, and then walking away thinking, "What's next?" I never celebrated earning my bachelor's degree because I was immediately focused on the next hoop: graduate school. And I got married the day after. My wife, Janice, and I set up house in a decrepit rental—barely more than a tenant shack—with odd redneck neighbors, archaic cast iron plumbing, a leaky gas heater that sometimes dangerously belched flames, and a combustible 1973 Ford Pinto that did double duty between Janice's trips to her nursing job and mine to school. There wasn't much money but we made things work in the way that young couples newly in love do. And then, within three months of our marriage, we were pregnant.

Whatever plans I've made in life—and there haven't been many—never included my having children of my own. When the pregnancy test came back baby-positive, my linear mind fractured into panicked pieces. How was I going to care for a child? I'd never fully fledged myself; I'd never lived alone, paid rent, made dinner for someone else, none of that. And here I was, suddenly deeper into life at twenty-three than most thirty-year-olds I knew. I woke one night soon after the revelation in the cold clammy sweat of a nightmare. Jesus—or someone in the costume of the Messiah—had showed up in the dream with some very practical questions. What would college tuition be like in 2008? Would this new, very unplanned thing in my life shortstop all the other things I had in fact dreamed of doing? I sat up straight in bed and shouted, "Jesus is all-powerful!"

The first pregnancy was a conversion of sorts. I didn't come back to Jesus; I leaned toward the philosophy that he was no god, but a martyr empowered by a couple thousand years of influence and tens of millions willing to pray, pilgrimage, judge, and slay in his name. But the coming of Baby Lanham still had me sending up these hypocritical nighttime hosannas. I was terrified. No longer would I be able to think solely about myself, or even about me and Janice as a couple. No, forevermore there would be this person that we'd created always attached, and for at least eighteen years tightly so. Nurses get paid well, but, I realized, I needed a job that would pay something beyond the five thousand dollars a year of my teaching assistantship. Jobs for zoologists, however, are few and far between. For those with only bachelor's degrees, they're almost nonexistent.

When I'd first changed my major from engineering, everyone had joked that I would become a zookeeper. Well they were right: I did. For almost a year I worked a part-time job at the Greenville Zoo, a small but popular facility only about an hour from where we lived. The position was as much an escape from the new stresses building in my life as work. I fell quickly into a Zen-like rhythm preparing daily diets for the animal collection and, as a zoo educator, hauling around a humongous boa constrictor and a cantankerous macaw. Between assigned duties, I assured appalled home-schooler moms, embarrassed teachers, and curious kids that the masturbating monkeys weren't doing anything out of the ordinary and no, we couldn't make them stop. We also couldn't make the ducks stop fucking one another. One amorous fulvous whistling duck just couldn't get enough of the hen ducks, and so when its corkscrew-like penis wouldn't retract and had to be surgically repaired, I was one of two keepers assigned to observe its behavior, a "duck dick watch." On many days I helped the elephant keeper shovel the amazing amount of shit that the single female pachyderm, Joy, left as a stinking, steaming overnight gift. Despite all this—and despite the terrible pay—the job was fun and the world was one where I felt at home and accepted.

Our daughter, Alexis, insisted on being born just six months in. With Janice on bed rest for twelve weeks, it was an additional stress to try to get an impatient fetus to hold on until properly ripened. We made it to thirty-six weeks and then our daughter wouldn't wait any longer. Suddenly, there was a tiny, squirming preemie dependent on decisions neither my wife nor I had ever made before. But most of my misgivings disappeared when I held her close to my chest for the first time and felt her little body warm against mine. It was instant love, and I resolved that we'd do whatever had to be done for her life to be as full and productive as we could make it. Baby Alexis made it through early struggles and I finished my master's degree in the midst of diaper changes, bottle feedings, crying bouts, giggling fits, first words and first steps. Once more I walked across a graduation stage and barely celebrated the achievement. With my family to consider, and shoveling shit not the best way to pay for a college education or even to help put groceries on the table, I was more focused on becoming a competent co-provider than on the addition of the two new letters to my résumé.

I'd been certified to teach high school biology and I halfheartedly pursued a couple of leads. But although Mama and Daddy had both been teachers, I didn't really want to stand in front of a classroom full of hormonally hyped adolescents. And birds were taking up less and less space in my life. Yes, there were moments here and there where my friends would coax me out for a few hours of birding. Two of them, much older white women, Jackie and JoAnne, would ask if I could "come out to play" with them. Another birding buddy, Vince Pack, was also a dependable diversion from Dad duty. We'd chase rarities here and there, but the bouts of birding seemed few and far between. I made lists of species I could see locally and wished for things further afield.

I moved on to a better-paying job that was less fun, at a wildlife toxicology research lab. They hired me to look for birds—dead ones that had succumbed to whatever pesticide had been applied. It was a morose task but I did it well. I was promoted from the field to the library and tasked with compiling the life histories of the birds most likely to be impacted by the chemicals agribusiness wanted to dump on crop fields. I spent hours in the stacks, leafing through journals and books. In the process of going through reams of literature, I discovered there were more questions than answers about common species we were supposed to know a lot about. I also discovered that I liked the detective work of uncovering gaps in knowledge.

I began to search for the next hoop. What would it be? There were job offers in wild places but without pulling my new family up by the roots in order for me to be a part-time spotted owl technician in the far reaches of the Pacific Northwest, or do bird census work in the cold climes of northernmost Wisconsin, I had few choices. Another degree seemed like the most sensible option; I would become J. Drew Lanham, PhD—Dr. Lanham. It also seemed like the most straightforward course through the next hoop. I'd seen fellow graduate students go on to doctoral work and it seemed to me just an extension of what I'd already done: more classes, more reading, more writing.

I was wrong. I struggled mightily for the next five years, as the hoop I'd thought I'd simply jump through like I had every other became menacingly smaller and sometimes burst into flames. My bird research project in the nearby Blue Ridge Mountains turned into a thick thorny tangle, constantly revealing new layers of complexity and logistical constraint that statistics didn't really want to solve. Days afield, armed with binoculars and data sheets, became wearisome. The transformation of the prairie warblers, yellow-breasted chats, and blue grosbeaks I'd cherished as a birder into data points, yielding no discernible answers for the questions I was asking, frustrated me to the point of depression. And then, in just the nick of time, our second child, Colby, came along. He was born in the middle of my dissertation-research blues, another unplanned distraction four years behind the first one. Unlike Alexis, Colby didn't want to come early, instead resisting entry into the cold world. When he finally emerged, I was just as in love as the first time. Another Lanham male on the earth.

Janice gained status as an RN and I earned more as a PhD student and worked part time as a biology instructor at a community college. Life moved forward. I recovered from the depression to finish my degree.

It's allegedly an academic taboo to receive all of your degrees from the same institution; to then teach at the same place is likened to academic incest. But when an opportunity arose to become faculty at Clemson, I took it. A few other schools had shown interest but Clemson's offer and proximity to home and family were too good a deal to pass up. And so I was suddenly a college professor. I jumped through the tenure-track hoops: gathering grants, publishing papers, teaching, and training graduate students. Early on, a few fellow faculty members told me that I'd never make it— that my hire had been strictly an affirmative action move and progression through the ranks would be all but impossible. In spite of their predictions I achieved status as a distinguished professor with an endowed chair and was named a master teacher. After twenty years things have mostly worked out professionally.

I didn't plan any of it. I just kept my eyes on the next hoop, then the next, then the next. Along the way, my family flourished, through good and bad times. Colby's diagnosis with epilepsy at thirteen years old wasn't planned. A string of family members dying—my father-in-law, my favorite uncle and aunt, all within a short span of years— wasn't planned. Hoops of assorted sizes keep presenting themselves. Some I can accurately gauge and calculate my leaps through; others are unpredictable and require gyrations and gymnastics. Gradually orthodoxy has ceded to the realizations that I'm responsible for my own happiness and my own destiny. I suppose life is the ultimate hoop we've all been challenged with jumping through.

What's next?

Birding While Black

Southern trees bear strange fruit,
Blood on the leaves and blood at the root.
— Abel Meeropol (aka Lewis Allan),
"Strange Fruit"

IT'S ONLY 9:06 A.M. AND I THINK I MIGHT GET HANGED TODAY.

The job I volunteered for was to record every bird I could see or hear in a three-minute interval. I am supposed to do that fifty times. Look, listen, and list for three minutes. Get in the car. Drive a half mile. Stop. Get out. Look, listen, and list again. It's a routine thousands of volunteers have followed during springs and summers all across North America since 1966. The data is critical for ornithologists to understand how breeding birds are faring across the continent.

Up until now the going has been fun and easy, more leisurely than almost any "work" anyone could imagine. But here I am, on stop number thirty-two of the Laurel Falls Breeding Bird Survey (BBS) route: a large black man in one of the whitest places in the state, sitting on the side of the road with binoculars pointed toward a house with the Confederate flag proudly displayed. Rumbling trucks passing by, a honking horn or two, and curious double takes are infrequent but still distract me from the task at hand. Maybe there's some special posthumous award given for dying in the line of duty on a BBS route—perhaps a roadside plaque honoring my bird-censusing skills.

My mind plays horrific scenes of an old black-and-white photograph I've seen before—gleeful throngs at a lynching party. Pale faces glow grimly in evil light. A little girl smiles broadly. The pendulant, black-skinned guest of dishonor swings anonymously, grotesquely, lifelessly. I can hear Billie Holiday's voice.

The mountain morning, which started out cool, is rapidly heating into the June swoon. I grip the clipboard tighter with sweaty hands, ignoring as best I can the stars and bars flapping menacingly in the yard across the road. The next three minutes will seem much longer.

On mornings like this I sometimes question why I choose to do such things. Was I crazy to take this route, up here, so far away from anything? What if someone in that house is not so keen on having a black man out here, maybe checking out things—or people—he shouldn't be? I've heard that some mountain folks don't like nosy outsiders poking around. Yet here I am, a black man birding.

⁓

Over the years I've listed hundreds of species in hundreds of places, from coast to coast and abroad, too. I've seen a shit-ton of birds from sea level to alpine tundra. But as a black man in America I've grown up with a profile. Society at large has certain boxes I'm supposed to fit into, and most of the labels on those boxes aren't good. Birders have a profile as well, a much more positively perceived one. Being a birder in the United States means that you're probably a middle-aged, middle-class, well-educated white man. While most of the labels apply to me, I am a black man and therefore a birding anomaly. The chances of seeing someone who looks like me while on the trail are only slightly greater than those of sighting an ivory-billed woodpecker. In my lifetime I've encountered fewer than ten black birders. We're true rarities in our own right.

⌒

For three years I've been responsible for this route, the only mountain BBS in the state. The scenery seemed worth the work. For good portions of the route the Blue Ridge Mountains crest the horizon. Birding in and out of open land and forests, with field sparrows bouncing songs off the broom sedge at one stop and hooded warblers blasting from a laurel-cloaked cove at the next, I sometimes have to pinch myself. Stop number twenty-four, beside an old apple orchard, is spectacular. Warbling blue grosbeaks, buzzing prairie warblers, and chattering yellow-breasted chats usually make the three minutes go by quickly. Earlier, when a lone bobwhite called from somewhere in the tangle of weeds and brush, I'd taken it as good omen for the day.

"Okay, 9:04. I need to start. A wood thrush—good, that's the first one for today. Summer tanager—no, scarlet tanager—two of 'em. American crows—sounds like maybe three of those . . ."

In the midst of ticking off species the thoughts begin to filter through my head again. Maybe these folks are the "heritage, not hate" type. I don't see any black lawn jockeys, wheelless cars hoisted up on cinder blocks, or rabid pit bulls in the yard. The only irritant beyond the flag is a persistently yapping Chihuahua, announcing my presence to anyone within earshot.

"OK. Was that a goldfinch singing from the top of that poplar?

Definitely goldfinch." A quick glance at my watch. I still have a full two minutes to go.

A yellow-billed cuckoo croaks from somewhere in the neighboring woodlot and I add it to the list. But I don't catch the next bird's call because I'm distracted. "Is somebody coming?" I imagine a scraggly haired hillbilly who is going to require things I'm unwilling to give. Past incidents don't fade quickly from memory, especially when the threats of danger were real, raising a sour-slick tang of bile in the back of my throat.

On one of my first jobs with the Department of Natural Resources, I thought my color would cost me my life. My supervisor, Kate, and I went out to deploy live traps for bats and small mammals up in the remote Jocassee Gorges, a maze of rhododendron-choked mountain coves, small streams, and pine-studded ridges. It's as close to wilderness as there is in the portion of the Upstate folks used to call the "Dark Corner."

I'd heard that people in the mountains didn't like strangers of any color. I was a strange stranger, and maybe not the person locals would think should be working with a white woman. Kate was a super-observant naturalist, who noticed the slightest nuances in tooth pattern or fur color—but was, I think, oblivious to the threat I perceived.

Riding on an old logging road just wide enough for one vehicle, we met another truck. The rusting, dented pickup's cab was full of three men. One of the vehicles would have to give way to the other on the narrow track, and so we pulled over. Kate and I each threw up a hand, offering the customary southern pickup-passerby wave. Their responses seemed halfhearted. Hardly a finger went up. Instead the men stared, heads slowly swiveling. Their looks bored through the windshield and wrapped themselves around my throat. The six eyes seemed to be making decisions I didn't want to be a part of.

I turned around as they rumbled by. Their brake lights suddenly flashed and the backup lights came on. The truck made a three-point turn for the only reason I could imagine: they'd decided that they didn't want us back there. My stomach knotted. I wondered how long it would take the authorities to recover our decomposing corpses from the rhododendron hells where these hillbillies would dump us after they did whatever the fuck it was they wanted to do. Kate nonchalantly wondered aloud at the trailing truck's intent but seemed more concerned that they'd maybe screwed with the pitfall traps we were going to check than about the prospect of impending assault.

I was on an edge that I'd only experienced in very bad dreams. The going was slow and the men followed us by a hundred yards or so. They kept pace, turn for turn. The knot in my belly tightened. We were on a dead-end road with no escape. We were unarmed. Without question the men in the truck would have guns and knives—probably a rope, too. For the first time in my newborn wildlife career I was questioning whether following my outdoor passion was truly worth it.

I'm not sure whether I prayed. Back then God was still an option in such circumstances. But whatever wish I threw out of the pickup window was granted. The trio stopped and turned around just as suddenly as they'd done in the first place. Kate drove on deeper into the gorge's maw and we worked into the evening, until darkness drove us from the woods. We didn't catch anything that day. I would've normally checked each trap with a Christmas-like anticipation, hoping some small critter—a smoky shrew, golden mouse, or red salamander—might be at the bottom of one of the five-gallon bucket traps.

That day, though, I couldn't have cared less. I worried over our exit. I was sure the men were just biding their time, lying in wait for us to come back out the only way we could. I fully expected to see them parked around every hairpin turn. I didn't relax until we hit the asphalt road that would take us home with speed. Kate told me later that she suspected the men in the truck thought we were law enforcement, maybe looking for marijuana patches or moonshine stills hidden in the woods.

In remote places fear has always accompanied binoculars, scopes, and field guides as baggage. A few years later, during my doctoral field research, three raggedy, red spray-painted *K*s appeared on a Forest Service gate leading to one of my study sites. When I saw the "welcome" sign, many of the old feelings came back. I instinctively looked over my shoulder to see if anyone was watching. And I didn't visit the point again. My safety compromised, I found another place to do the science. I'd had to do this a couple of years earlier, too, when a white supremacist group "organized" in the mountains of western North Carolina, near the places I was supposed to do a research project. They'd made the national news in stories that showed them worshipping Hitler and shooting at targets that looked like Martin Luther King Jr. Someone at the university joked about my degree being awarded posthumously. So though the proposal had been written and the project was well on its way to being funded—and as potentially groundbreaking the research on rose-breasted grosbeaks, golden-winged warblers, and forest management in the Southern Appalachians might be—I had abandoned the whole thing.

These decisions put doubts about my dedication to the field in my head. After all, I was in wildlife biology, a profession where work in remote places is often an expectation. Any credibility I was trying to build would be shattered if I showed hesitation in venturing out beyond some negro-safe zone of comfort. And so I mostly swallowed the fear, adjusted when I had to, and moved on.

I'm not alone, though. I have friends—black friends—who've also experienced the lingering looks, the stares of distaste. They've endured comments about their color flung within earshot. I look at maps through this lens—at the places where tolerance seems to thrive, and where hate and racism seem to fester—and think about where I want to be. Mostly those places jibe with my desire to be in the wild but sometimes they don't.

The wild things and places belong to all of us. So while I can't fix the bigger problems of race in the United States—can't suggest a means by which I, and others like me, will always feel safe—I can prescribe a solution in my own small corner. Get more people of color "out there." Turn oddities into commonplace. The presence of more black birders, wildlife biologists, hunters, hikers, and fisherfolk will say to others that we, too, appreciate the warble of a summer tanager, the incredible instincts of a whitetail buck, and the sound of wind in the tall pines. Our responsibility is to pass something on to those coming after. As young people of color reconnect with what so many of their ancestors knew—that our connections to the land run deep, like the taproots of mighty oaks; that the land renews and sustains us—maybe things will begin to change.

I'm hoping that soon a black birder won't be a rare sighting. I'm hoping that at some point I'll see color sprinkled throughout a birding-festival crowd. I'm hoping for the day when young hotshot birders just happen to be black like me. These hopes brighten the darkness of past experiences. The present does, too. What I've learned from all the years of looking for birds in far-flung places and expecting the worst from people is that my assumptions are more times than not unfounded. These nature-seeking souls are mostly kindred spirits, out to find not just birds but solace. A catalog of friends—most of them white—have inspired, guided, and sometimes even nurtured my passion for birds and nature. As we gaze together, everything that's different about us disappears into the plumages of the creatures we see beyond our binoculars. There is power in the shared pursuit of feathered things.

Forty-five more seconds and I will be done. An ovenbird singing over there. A northern cardinal chipping. And human eyes on me. I can feel them watching. This last minute is taking forever. The little mutt is barking like it's rabid. I don't hear or see any birds in the last thirty seconds because I am watching the clock tick down. Time's up! I collect my fears and drive the next half mile, on to stop number thirty-three.

Jawbone

One does not hunt in order to kill; on the contrary, one
kills in order to have hunted.

⟶ José Ortega y Gasset,
Meditations on Hunting

Killing is a dying art. In a shrink-wrapped, prepackaged
world, most people don't consider or want to know where their
meat comes from. They willfully ignore the connection between
the preformed patties and poultry nuggets bought at the drive-
through and a hormonally "enhanced" steer standing knee deep
in manure or a genetically modified hen whose fast-forwarded life
was constrained to a tiny crate. We grill, stew, fry, and chew through
animal flesh as if nothing had to die for it.

But I'm a hunter. I watch and wait. I savor the stalk. I aim, exhale,
and tense trigger finger to send fast lead to quick ethical end. I want
to understand the world that I share with prey and other predators. I
hunt because it sustains. Hunting is food for my soul. If I've studied,
noticed, and guessed right, and my aim is true, it provides meat for
the body, too.

Unlike many of my hunting friends, I didn't learn from a
father or uncle. Although Daddy would occasionally bring a rabbit
home for dinner, our real meat supply was grazing in the pasture

or rooting in the pigpen. The need for protein was mostly met by things that lived behind barbed wire and at the feed trough.

As a kid I fantasized about hunting. After killing the sparrow with my BB gun, I made a few forays afield with the single-shot .410, but they were largely unsuccessful and unfocused. Maybe the sparrow's death lingered with me; killing simply for the sake of killing wasn't right. Later in life, as a college zoology major and then as an ornithology graduate student, hunting or killing didn't seem acceptable unless the dead things would end up stuffed with cotton and laid out on a museum tray. As a budding ornithologist I was "armed" only with a field guide and binoculars. Guns and camouflage didn't fit the birder gestalt. And some of the birders didn't have particularly nice things to say about hunters or hunting. Hunters were "Bubbas," or "rednecks," who took more than they gave. Even the wildlife biologists on the other side of campus were called "Bubba biologists"—pseudoscientists without the brains or sophistication to do real research or move conservation forward in a thoughtful way.

But I remembered Mr. Ferguson and Mr. Sharpe, the two men that Daddy had trusted to hunt on the Home Place. They had respected the land and seemed bent more on pursuing than killing. The chance to learn more came with a change in professional focus. As I left the undergraduate and master's degrees in zoology for a doctorate in forestry and wildlife, I was suddenly in a different world. I, too, was a "Bubba biologist." And I liked what I saw, and how I felt. In this new world, application was just as important as knowledge. In their pragmatic universe, my colleagues sometimes promoted legally sanctioned, ethical killing of designated game animals to relieve an overburdened landscape. These folks were just as adept at identifying fall warblers and talking about predator-prey dynamics as the zoologists, but they stressed that things had to get done on the ground for anything to get "saved."

I learned that saving things required real money, as well as management theory that was tested and retested. I discovered that hunters' guns, ammunition, bows, arrows, and licenses all fed cash back into conservation coffers. I learned that most of the camouflage-wearing gun toters were ethical people doing something practical for conservation. In the long run, they saved more lives than they took. The sense of it won me over. The meat-sharing kindness of hunter friends and peers helped, too. The locally gathered venison was delicious.

My transition from a wine-drinking, cheese-eating ecologist to a beer-swilling, venison-chewing wildlife biologist came in my late twenties, as I moved closer to becoming Dr. Lanham. I now had the time and the deepening desire to get out and learn. I crept from the camo-less closet, purchasing a rifle, practicing shooting, and following friends and mentors into the woods. I sat for hours, days, and years before even seeing my first deer. This seemed almost impossible—deer teemed from every corner of every forest and field and spilled into yards and onto roadsides and highways—but as I sat high in tree stands for several years in beautiful autumn woods, watching the wild world pass by, I saw everything except deer. But although I came home empty-handed, I was full hearted. The wildlife I witnessed and the peace and solitude of the pursuit honed skills of observation and patience. When I finally killed my first deer, a yearling doe, on the edge of a Lowcountry field in the last few minutes of the waning day, my hunter's heart was blooded. In the same way a warm smear of red is smudged across a new hunter's face on his or her first kill, my soul was marked deep. The deer was small, a lithe thing. There were no antlers to hang as a trophy or heavy weight to brag about. But there was a life gone, which I'd taken and which I honored by consuming the flesh that had once run and leapt.

Still, I think about hunting more than I hunt. In a July swelter I wish for cold mornings and clear November skies studded with stars, for making my way through quiet woods to climb high. I can remember hundreds of hunts and recall moments from almost every one. There are scenes, scents, sounds, and sentiments that run rapid-fire when any one of a thousand memories is triggered—by, for example, the jawbone that hangs on my office wall.

The jawbone is more than just a memento of a particular hunt. Running my fingers over the deer's flattened, paddle-like incisors inspires thoughts of all the tendrils of greenbrier he once nipped in the spring. The ridges on the molars are worn down to a thin wall of dull white enamel, giving way to the dark-brown dentin that thickens with age. The result of years of grinding acorns and beechnuts and regurgitating cud, the wear tells the story of an old animal. I've estimated that the jawbone belonged to a whitetail going into the sixth year of his life.

If the wildlife biologists are to be believed, a single adult white-tailed deer (*Odocoileus virginianus*) can consume about seven pounds of food each day. That means the jawbone in my hands had chewed close to seven tons of vegetation, including the leaves and shoots of dozens of kinds of grasses, forbs, vines, shrubs, and trees, along with bushels of tart persimmons from a dry ridge, sweet blackberries from a cutover, pulpy pawpaws from a creek bottom, and crunchy beechnuts and acorns. Including a second effort with cud, the teeth had undergone countless masticulations.

Deer, like other cud chewers, evolved a rapid-eating strategy to have a better chance of not being caught by some long-toothed, sharp-clawed predator. As most things consistently capable of catching adult deer have been exterminated, human predators have come to present the most persistent predatory challenge to white-tails. In expensive camouflage clothing and toting high-tech bows, high-caliber rifles, can't-miss calls, irresistible attractant scents, and other snake-oil guarantees to magically lure deer, legions of hunters clamber into the woods with limited time, itchy trigger fingers, and "hornographic" wet dreams of big-antlered glory. Some of them blaze away at anything remotely resembling a deer. For many deer hunters, "If it's brown, it's down" is the seasonal maxim.

When my friend Ralph Costa and I reclaimed Mama's family's land, the Ninety Six Home Place, we aimed to build a hunting place where all wildlife could flourish. A covey or two of bobwhite quail lived on the property and I knew that trees would have to be cut and fire introduced to hold onto them. But there were constant challenges. Trespassers. Poachers. And night-riding spotlight-ers, who shot deer blinded with high-intensity beams. For several years we would return to the property to prepare for the coming season only to find young bucks poached and destroyed by people who believed the land and the deer on it belonged to them. The carcass, left to rot at the property gate with its antlers sawn off, sent a message that the "No Trespassing" signs didn't matter. These weren't hunters. They were slobs giving hunting a bad name.

Every year in a white-tailed deer's life is a gamble. That fact makes the bony remains in my grasp even more precious. Holding this jawbone—part of an animal that somehow grew from a spot-ted, spindly legged fawn to a master of the woods, in spite of all the things that nature and humans have to dish out—is a minor miracle. More amazing is the fact that for all of the wariness and instinct honed over those five-plus years and 128 acres on the Ninety Six

Home Place, the buck's life ended at my hands instead of someone
else's. I can't count that as blind coincidence. If blessings can come
from beasts then this was one.

⁓

On the day the jawbone came into my possession, I raced against
the breaking dawn to make it into the woods. Ignoring an old
tunneled-in logging road for a new and more convenient sit, I
strode as quickly and quietly into the woods as I could. The stars
were already fading. I walked for a quarter mile and climbed into a
ladder stand propped against a tall scarlet oak. A skid trail passed
from east to west beneath me. I'd purposely had the woodland avenue put in during the last logging operation, to provide a shortcut
between the clear-cut and the piedmont prairie glade. I'd suspected that the cutover, dog-hair thick with hardwood saplings,
briar tangles, and an assortment of weeds and grasses, was deer
heaven. I closed my eyes to enjoy the remains of the darkness and
let the world wake up around me.

I settled in. The deer apparently did, too, wherever they were.
Still, among the periodic bouts of napping, bird-watching, and day-
dreaming, I saw a menagerie of wild things to occupy the deer-
lessness. The usual suspects: gray squirrels, overachieving towhees,
white-throated sparrows, and even a pair of coyotes—one gorgeous
blond male and a stunning jet-black bitch.

I grunted and bleated from time to time, doing my best imitation of a buck and a doe in serious sexual negotiation. Patience
waned with the fourth hour in the stand and my guard dropped.
As autumn color rained down, I was lost in the beauty of the place
that my mother's mother and father once nurtured. I relaxed in

other thoughts—and with that calming, the adrenaline that poisons the woods with predatory scent dissipated. My mind was drifting further and further away from the present when suddenly there was a crash I immediately knew to be different. Trees and limbs don't fall with heavy purpose. Whatever had created the noise was big, and moving with more than gravity as its impetus. I refocused and regathered predatory intent. I pushed a call through my tube.

In the middle of my sputtering and grunting something that looked like a dun-colored horse exploded from the dense cover between the oak swale and the clear-cut. All I could see were splotches of brown appearing and disappearing between the trunks of trees. I couldn't label it buck or doe but I knew it was a deer—moving fast and maybe eighty or a hundred yards in front of me. I'm not sure a curse made it past my lips but I was thinking in four-letter code. This thing was in a hurry to be somewhere else. As it finally broke into the clearing all of the puzzle pieces came together in the frame of a huge whitetail buck that was gathering up ten yards of ground with each powerful stride. I saw a shoulder, a muscle-bound neck, and a head crowned with antlers. I grunted again, louder. The buck didn't stop. The last I glimpsed of the biggest deer I'd ever seen was a white rear disappearing as fast as the front had come into view.

My heart raced at about the same speed that the deer had galloped. The buck was gone. I remembered to breathe and tried to regain some semblance of calm as I sank back into my seat. My hands trembled and my mouth was sandy dry. Had I imagined what I'd just seen?

There are always moments of regathering after a close encounter with a wild thing like this. You question your place in the chain of being. I've been out west, birding in places where cougars prowl, and looked over my shoulder more than once thinking I heard—or felt—something following me. African lions roaring under the stars of the Southern Cross in the Kalahari Desert made me feel small, insignificant, and grateful for our encampment's walls. A few days on Kodiak Island, a spectacular place "infested" with giant brown bears at the rate of one per square mile, gave me and my friend Lane pause in going anywhere alone. Of course large predators, things that could easily kill and eat you, don't exist on the Ninety Six property. But sometimes even the smallest hunters can captivate and intimidate. One morning a sharp-shinned hawk landed close enough for me to see the wildness flickering in its eyes. A forest-darting, bird-killing flying machine, I saw at close quarters the deadly tools the little "blue-darter" deals: a beak hooked and sharpened for tearing, long-taloned toes for puncturing and gripping, and a long narrow tail for ruddering through thick woods. The little raptor's gaze caught mine and I felt as small in that moment as a chickadee or kinglet whose dodging wasn't quick enough to make the next instant. Now the buck's appearance had left me feeling awed and tiny, too.

As my heartbeat leveled off and the shaking subsided, I marveled in the fact that after all the years of walking Ninety Six, the art and science of well-thought-out management had somehow paid off. I'd respected the home of Mama's folks. I'd previously seen scrapes, rubs, cow-sized tracks, and split-second glimpses of a huge form leaping the span of the road, indications of a mature deer's presence. The sighting now of this almost mythical animal was a validation of my care. I decided I'd sit for a little longer, to let things settle again.

Just as I had resigned the brief encounter to blind luck that I might never experience again, a purposeful crack in the deadfall behind me stopped my heart. Turning slowly I caught a glimpse of tawny brown. And then there was a flickering ear, and an eye—a wide, blinking eye. Nose to the ground, the buck made his way toward the avenue, grunting softly.

The wind in my face was now in the buck's nose. It was a magnet drawing him to what I'm sure he hoped was a doe ready to begin the next generation. I sat up in the stand, afraid to move or even blink, as the buck angled toward an old stump where I'd left some drops of scent earlier. What had been almost an afterthought was now the only thing on the buck's mind.

In those moments when an animal like a mature whitetail, buck or doe, graces your presence, you and the deer match wits. The hunter possesses an alleged intelligence and a tool fashioned with opposable thumbs—sharpened stick, chert arrow, or high-powered rifle—that makes killing a technically easier thing. But the deer holds all the sensory advantages.

There's an edge conferred to wild things that bypasses the technical and often defeats hot powder and hard bullet, sharp arrow and taut string. Whitetails, wild turkeys, and every other wild being seem to possess a sixth sense. They know when you are there, seem to calculate your next move, and maneuver to avoid it. You're playing checkers; they're playing chess. Maybe it's the acrid stink of stress on the wind or the drumbeats inside the hunter's chest that send warning rhythms to the hunted. So many times that final half step or quarter turn required for a clean killing shot don't happen before a flagging whitetail bounds away. You're left disappointed but somehow also joyfully overcome and filled with gratitude—reminded of the importance of breath, heartbeats, and instinct.

That morning, though, the buck didn't trust his built-in advantages. Urge overcame caution. His big head and broad shoulders slid behind an oak. Hidden from one another for that brief second, I shifted, shouldered the rifle, and steadied as he emerged on the other side of the tree, thirty yards away. I didn't dare breathe. As I positioned the scope's crosshairs on the deer's shoulder, it was hard to keep anything steady. I bleated weakly, my best try at a young doe wanting his attention. He threw his head up immediately and looked at and through me.

I could not say what, if anything, that whitetail thought in that instant of recognition. I do suspect that in that moment, he came to his wood sense again, but got stuck between trusting his nose and ears and believing what he saw. For deer, the maxim of believing half of seeing and none of hearing is reversed. Scent and sound overrode sight, for just an instant. It was long enough for me to make a decision for us both.

In the second it took for me to admire his power, his beauty, his grace, his powerful presence, I pressed my cheek into the gunstock and the unsteady crosshairs settled cleanly. The abrupt intersection of the buck's searching and my seeking was on a quarter-sized spot of dun-brown hide, heart-lung high.

I don't remember shooting. But in the combination of trigger squeeze, rifle report, and recoil, bullet was sent toward target. With the shot the buck recollected the wild gallop I'd seen when he first exploded from the place he now seemed hell-bent on returning to. He dug in hard, trying to gain a foothold on the soft loam that lined the freshly plowed roadbed. In what seemed like minutes but was more likely less than a second or two he raced away like a thoroughbred horse out of the gate, bounding over a maze of fallen timber. There was no telltale crash to end the story. Maybe all I'd done was to educate him by a bullet's breadth to be wiser.

I was shaking again. My hands trembled. The .270 almost

slipped from my grip and I felt weak, as if every bit of energy in me had exploded out of the gun's barrel with the 150-grain bullet. Cursing, I unloaded and lowered my rifle to the ground on the safety line and climbed down behind it. My legs noodled and I nearly fell off the last few rungs of the ladder. On the ground I collected my nerves and paced to the spot where I hoped to find blood. I looked where the buck had stood but found none. Had I somehow missed this deer, at less than fifty paces?

Blood would've been almost instantly obvious on the thickening layer of dead leaves and green carpet of clover. I walked in circles but couldn't find a single drop. There were tracks, though, large ones. They looked more like something a fat steer would've left than a whitetail. I followed the evidence of his violent tear back into the sparse oak woods, thinking that maybe I'd need to find a wounded animal. A liver shot could lead an animal to wander, dying slowly. It could linger for hours, suffering in some impenetrable thicket.

A shaking, self-doubting mess, I walked slowly and thought carefully about what had just happened. Five steps into the woods and still no blood. The doubt swelled to despair. I looked through the brush and tree trunks hoping to see a telltale white belly on the forest floor. A few more steps. All I saw were leaves—dry, brown leaves. Then I knelt and looked at something different. There, like a tiny stop sign, was a fingernail-sized spot of life. It was brilliantly vermilion; lungs or heart were pierced. Wherever the buck was, its life was fated to end. I rubbed the greasy redness between my fingers and walked a few feet further. The blood was suddenly everywhere, painting the brown-and-yellow forest floor in life's ending.

I could feel a presence somewhere close. From the last eruption of blood, sprayed across a fallen log, I looked up to see the big buck once again. He lay facing me. His front legs were folded neatly underneath him and his head was held high by a tangle of wild grapevines among his antlers. I stopped. He didn't look finished. Out of habit I'd rechambered a round once I was safely on the ground. I brought the rifle up now, expecting the deer to spring to his feet and bolt away. But when I stepped forward, it was clear that the buck was dead.

I knelt and felt the muscled power beneath the thick gray-brown coat, and the warmth of life cooling quickly away. I touched the stone-smooth coldness of the broad, cedar-stained antlers. I prayed to something for the luck and thanked the buck for his existence, given now to mine.

Antlers are a coveted trophy. They represent seasons ruled over a deep wood, high ridge, or dark swamp. That majesty—sometimes stolen by poachers and cheaters but hard earned by those in a fair chase—is certainly a worthy remembrance of encounters afield.

I was drawn, however, to the worn teeth of the animal whose life I had ended. There was so much more than antlers that he died for. The almost eighty pounds of venison nourished family and friends for the next two years. Life sustains life, something I've learned watching the world wake up from high in a pine and feeling the pounding of my heart when a wary creature walks unknowing and close enough for me to feel the wildness.

Many vegetarians claim that their heads lie easier at night knowing that they've inflicted no killing or suffering. But the soybeans that yield tofu have to grow somewhere, and it's not all in hydroponic, solar-powered hothouses. No, the neat and tidy rows of soybeans and amber waves of grain grow in fields that used to be wildlife habitat. These crops do indeed bear the blood, but differently: in altered habitat, displaced wildlife, chemical runoff, transportation costs, and greenhouse gases emitted in food conversion. The ethics of food are never uncomplicated.

The teeth that few would have chosen as a trophy represent much more to me than antlers ever could. It is more than a single deer that I hold in my hand, more than five years of liberty and wildness. This jawbone represents a connection to place and time that supersedes years, acreage, and antler size. The worn teeth represent the history of what has been and are a sign of what might be. This jawbone—in many ways—is me.

New Religion

It is not half so important to know as to feel.

⟶ Rachel Carson,
The Sense of Wonder

LECTURING HAS ALWAYS COME EASILY TO ME. BACKED BY THE technical, the theoretical, a few supporting slides, and a captive audience of college students or peers, I've given hundreds of presentations in classrooms and professional meetings. But after many years of stale introductions, methods, results, and conclusions, I began to wonder if anyone was listening—and if there was real reason for them to. In lecture after lecture I regurgitated factoids and data that were readily available in the readings. And between the slides of animals on the verge of extinction and of tropical rainforests being slashed, burned, and mowed down by cattle, I sounded to my own ears like the apocalyptic preachers at Jeter Baptist Church. I looked into my audience and saw drawn expressions of boredom and dread.

Day after day, semester after semester, year after year, I droned on. Yes, I was presenting the facts. Yes, I was publishing the facts. But it seemed to me that the facts never created motivation to make things better. Conservation to me had always implied caring, some semblance of selflessness for those coming after. I craved change but wasn't quite sure where or how to satisfy that desire.

In the midst of this yearning, I took a group of graduate students to Warren Wilson, a small, "working-hands" liberal arts college in the mountains of western North Carolina, to see the preeminent conservation biologist E. O. Wilson speak. I'm not a star chaser but Dr. Wilson, a fellow southerner and naturalist, is a supernova, a once-in-a-generation mind whose ideas shine like the sun in the conservation world. He introduced the ideas of biodiversity and biophilia to the world. He's on par with Aldo Leopold and Rachel Carson. I didn't want to miss the chance to see him, and some of the students felt the same.

As we gathered in the chapel that night the pews were overflowing. We found a few vacant spots on the floor in front. Dr. Wilson—a tall, slim, gray-haired grandfather of a man—soon emerged and mounted a pulpit that looked like the bow of a ship. Standing above but almost within the audience, he spoke softly of the need to notice nature. There weren't any statistics, graphs, or scatterplots. There were no slides or pictures of devastated forests and animals dying in traps. His voice, even amplified through a microphone, never rose above the quiet surge of low-tide surf. Yet he was irresistibly compelling, magnetic. I was entranced. I looked around—everyone else was drawn in, too. There were nods of approval, and more than a few eyes glistened with tears. It was church like I'd never imagined it. There was no damnation or guilt, but simply a heart-filled plea to notice, nurture, and care.

After the talk I approached Dr. Wilson to thank him for sharing his brilliance and ask for an autograph. I don't recall much of what he said, but I do remember the deepest, kindest gaze. It was a caring look that made me feel singular in a room full of admirers. In my book he drew a tiny ant alongside his signature. Just as that creature had sparked his great passions, that evening planted a seed of what might be in me.

A few years later, I spent several springs in northern Vermont, writing and thinking about nature in a different way. In that strange place my right brain flickered back on. The need to impress other professors, pile up peer-reviewed publications, and cache grant dollars began to give way to a desire for consciousness. Vermont was the greenest place I'd ever been. It was also a place where no one knew me. In that freedom my stress-tightened shoulders dropped and the tension in my jaw lessened. I slowed down and walked dirt roads—sometimes barefoot and empty minded, with not much more in my head than the present moment. Warbling vireos and least flycatchers were the only audiences I entertained.

Within the past couple of years I've given fewer and fewer "p-value" presentations. More and more I find myself taking the hard data and wrapping it in genuine caring. The science is critical; it is the "scripture." It always comes first. But action has to come behind it. I try to "connect the conservation dots." Aldo Leopold's admonitions to be one of those who "cannot live without wild things"; to "keep all the parts," "listen to the mountain," and "preserve the integrity, stability, and beauty of the biotic community" fly round and round inside me like swifts swirling before the roost. The words are flocks of inspiration that I want to migrate from my mouth into the heads and hearts of others. I shake hands less now and give hugs more. I exchange more heartbeats than business cards. The energy is palpable. I can feel the brackish bay-marsh tide rising and the prairie winds sweeping through crowds that crave it. I can see the full moon's glow in kindred eyes.

If teaching is preaching, I've become a warmer, gentler pastor, more like the clergy at Mt. Canaan. Maybe it's appropriate that these years have given me new spiritual release, too. I've settled into a comfortable place with the idea of nature and god being the same thing. Evolution, gravity, change, and the dynamic transformation of field into forest move me. A warbler migrating over hundreds of miles of land and ocean to sing in the same tree once again is as miraculous to me as any dividing sea. Doing good things for and revering nature are just acts. There is righteousness in conserving things, staving off extinction, and simply admiring the song of a bird. In my moments of confession in front of strangers, talking about my love of something much greater than any one of us, I become a freer me. Each time I am reborn.

For all those years of running from anything resembling religion and all the scientific training that tells me to doubt anything outside of the prescribed confidence limits, I find myself defined these days more by what I cannot see than by what I can. As I wander into the predawn dark of an autumn wood, I feel the presence of things beyond flesh, bone, and blood. My being expands to fit the limitlessness of the wild world. My senses flush to full and my heartbeat quickens with the knowledge that I am not alone.

Thinking

Nothing is more beautiful than the loveliness of the
woods before sunrise.

⌐ George Washington Carver

I THINK ABOUT LAND A LOT. IN FACT, I AM POSSESSED BY IT.

I think about the lay of the land, how it came to be, what natural forces have changed it, what human forces have mangled it, how concrete and asphalt doom it. I think about the promise it holds for the future and what history it preserves from the past. I think about how it rises and runs, lifts and falls. I think about hills and hollows. I think about great rifts and grand canyons. I think about mountains and monadnocks. I think about swamps and sandhills. I think about draws and drains. I think about the rivers running through land, the animals burrowing under it, and the birds flying over it. I think about the sounds that come from the land: the whining of katydids and crickets on steamy summer nights, the incessant serenading of red-eyed vireos on newborn spring days, and the chattering of squirrels hiding acorns on chill-crisped autumn mornings. I think about clapper rails applauding at the edge of a salt marsh stage and the teletyping dictations of pinewoods tree frogs in a rain-soaked longleaf savannah. I think about the solace of winter whispered on a northwest wind and the mournful groaning of the bare-boned trees. I think about the soil underneath it all: its shifting sandiness, rough rockiness, rich loaminess, and sticky clayeyness. I think about the perfume of place: the pleasant mustiness of decaying leaves on a Blue Ridge forest floor, the sulfur stink of a Beaufort mudflat at low tide, the drunken sweetness of an orchard in October.

I think about mountains. I've been moved to tears by the stark beauty of snowcapped peaks touching heaven. Those western mountains are young, brash spires—bragging and daring us to confront the impossibility of their being. But in my native South Carolina, the mountains are humble beings. They're less boastful, worn down by the pressures of time and weather. I see their rounded shoulders as a testament to persistence and the inevitability of change, which wears granite and gneiss and quartz to sand and soil.

A two-lane highway—once an American Indian path—that winds like a blacksnake through an Upstate valley called Oolenoy lets the lazy wonder from afar. The stone-bare faces of Table Rock and Caesar's Head are enough for those in a hurry. The road leads to places with interesting names—Sunset, Pumpkintown, and Tigerville—quaint in the ways you'd expect. There are things to buy and maybe things to see. But I think too much about what lies beyond these snares. I see the Blue Wall and want to push past comfort. And so I go into the mountains from time to time, invading their dim coves and caverns. I cannot see the pinnacles in these places, cannot worship the horizons they make. Where poplar, basswood, hemlock, and rhododendron filter the light to almost constant dusk, I am consumed, swallowed whole in awe. I settle into places with old names like Jocassee, Keowee, Eastatoe, the Horse Pasture, and Musterground. I think about what used to be there: flocks of green-and-gold Carolina parakeets roosting in the cavernous hollows of monstrous yellow poplars, cool creeks running unimpeded by progress, no lakeshore real estate or exclusive gated communities with names made up to sound wild.

In the spring, the newness of things up on the edge of the Blue Ridge still overwhelms. Rebirth and renewal are clichés but speak truth anyway. Come summer I am devoured by remnant forests that from far away look uniformly verdant but from within are every shade of green imaginable. In autumn, death and departing are everywhere as canopies fall to the ground in pieces and birds look further south. Winter's starkness—a drab gray and brown outlined against the suddenly there sky, like pen and ink on ragmade paper—leads me into melancholy and a sense of being that's deep rooted. In the belly of a Blue Wall forest, every season howls through the hollows and rolls over the hills with a clarity that cries out for worship. I know that I'm in the depths of a living, breathing thing.

I leave the mountains and find the land at the foot of the Blue Wall. I think about the piedmont as I roller-coaster up and down through it. Rolling, undulating, ridge and valley, hill and slope. Things are in pieces here, fragments of what used to be. A bit of forest, a bit of field, a wetland rarely—all surrounded by a sea of cement. Acres and acres of asphalt. Even where I find forest, the trees are often planted like row crops. Elsewhere the loblolly pines have crept like weeds over the landscape. Invaders planted out of desperation and gone wild, they held some of the soil on the old fields so that it didn't all wash away to the sea. In most places, the thin crust of topsoil that remains struggles to hide the gummy clay underneath. When the infrequent rains do come, the Midlands weep erosively.

I think about the oak and hickory that used to be here. I think about the squirrels and blue jays that spread the seeds of the forest and the white-tailed deer and wild turkeys that are thankful for an acorn bounty. In spring I think about the vireos and warblers, and the gobblers that give me the slip on April mornings. In fall I imagine big bucks rubbing cedars on the dim edge of dawn and hermit thrushes settling into the same thicket at eventide. There are Edens to be found in piedmont paradises lost.

As things roll up and down, they will eventually flatten. Ancient dunes, sand, and pine and scrub oak creep in. On the sandhills and in the flatwoods below them, I think about gopher tortoises, which patiently share their burrows with other species, while Bachman's sparrows sing sweetly in the colonnades of old-growth longleaf. Maybe some of those big trees are rendering sap like candles. Or perhaps they are pockmarked with perfect holes holding the next generation of red-cockaded woodpeckers.

The once expansive swath of longleaf and wire grass woodland is mostly gone—cut down, covered over, and converted. Neither gopher tortoises nor Bachman's sparrows nor red-cockaded wood-peckers find safe haven in concrete and condominiums. I think about the tragedy in all that loss, and wonder how much of it we'll be able to salvage.

I think about the land as I speed by it on busy interstates. Driving at hyperspeed on a four-lane highway to someplace bet-ter leaves very little time for looking beyond a blurry wall of trees. Headed downhill from Upcountry to Low the land falls away from the road at the mercy of water: creek, river, swamp, marsh, and ulti-mately ocean. Here and there I glimpse the trees that tell me where the water stands. Cypress, sycamore, and willow like the wet places. Sand slowly gives way to silt. Things bottom out the further south I go and in the lowest places the water will sit if not drained or diverted or dammed.

The very highway I fly on to get somewhere unimportant really fast is often the dike itself, separating one part of the world from the other. It is also murderer's row for many four-legged creatures.

But in spite of the engineering, the water flows sluggishly. And even when it appears to stagnate, it cooks a wondrous stew of living things. Whirligig beetles dance on the tea-stained surface. Nervous mosquito fish dart away from shadows where bowfin lurk. As I drive by, the gaps in the green wall reveal feathered statues: egrets and herons, maybe a wood stork or two. I imagine alligators cruising in the depths and snapping turtles lying in wait.

Remembering, dreaming, contemplating, even commiserating—land is always somehow on my mind. I think this is because I'm missing the land from which I came; the pastures, fields, woods, creeks, and bottoms of my Home Place. My obsession is born of the land in Edgefield that nurtured me—land in the middle of nowhere that meant everything to me. It is born of growing up on garden-raised vegetables, pasture-fed beef, and the sweet fruits of our own orchards. It is born of some of the best years of my life.

It is born of my ancestors' sweat equity. These ancestors toiled on the land as enslaved Africans, eventually owned some of it, and then gave away many of its riches for pennies on the dollar. It is born of my frustration with fragmented farms and the families whose lives would be more whole if their land was, too.

But then again, maybe I think too much about black folks denying their kinship to country—not Mother Africa, but our country here. Backwoods, dirt road, deeply dark, pinpricked with stars at night: who-gives-a-damn-if-you-piss-in-your-own-backyard, hair-raising-hoot-owl country.

I don't expect everyone to feel the same way that I do about land. For so many of us, the scars are still too fresh. Fields of cotton stretching to the horizon—land worked, sweated, and suffered over for the profit of others—probably don't engender warm feelings among most black people. But the land, in spite of its history, still holds hope for making good on the promises we thought it could, especially if we can reconnect to it. The reparations lie not in what someone will give us, but in what we already own. The land can grow crops for us as well as it does for others. It can yield loblolly pine and white oak for us as it has for others. And it can nurture wildlife and the spirit for us, just like it has for others.

Place and land and nature: how we tie these things together is critical to our sense of self-purpose and our fit in the world. They are the trinity. This is true for people everywhere, but nowhere is it truer than in the South.

Follow the ribbon of Interstate 95 in South Carolina that stretches from the southernmost tip of the state and parallels the coast to the North Carolina line. Beyond the beauty of moss-draped bald cypress wetlands and deep, dark pine forests, below the slow-beating wings of angel-white egrets and an invisible god, thousands of people can't afford a square foot of the soil that their ancestors paid for with their lives. These people sit tantalizingly close to wealth many of their kindred owned before it was taken away or lost. St. Helena Island, near Hilton Head, stands largely alone as an exception, with much of the land still in black hands and the African culture of its Gullah residents nationally treasured.

For too many, though, third world poverty is the shameful inheritance shared along this corridor. Barely potable water, substandard health care and schools, and land languishing in mismanagement define everyday life here. The government subsidies that pay people to grow trees, protect wetlands, or manage wildlife bypass most of the black landowners. As wealth whizzes by in a luxury sedan at ninety miles an hour, many see any hope speeding by, too.

I've been all over the world, now, but my wanderlust seems to always find its way home to piedmont clay, loblolly pine, and prairie warblers. And though I can't be at the Home Place, I've been lucky. I have land, and I think about it. I think about quail calling in the pines that I've just thinned. I think about hunting lovesick turkeys in the alley between the cutover and the creek bottom. I think about the comfort of eating food that comes by my own hand and hard work. I imagine the forty acres and the swayback mules so many were promised but never got.

And so I think about land. But more and more I also think about how other black and brown folks think about land. I wonder how our lives would change for the better if the ties to place weren't broken by bad memories, misinformation, and ignorance. I think about schoolchildren playing in safe, clean, green spaces, where the water and air flow clear and the birdsong sounds sweet. More and more I think of land not just in remote, desolate wilderness but in inner-city parks and suburban backyards and community gardens. I think of land and all it brings in my life. I think of land and hope that others are thinking about it, too.

Digging

It is no use asking me or any one else how to dig. . . . Better
go and watch a man digging, and then take a spade and
try to do it.

— Gertrude Jekyll,
Wood and Garden

THERE ARE MISSING LINKS IN EVERY FAMILY CHAIN, INCLUDING
that of our great, global family. In 1974, anthropologists dug the
petite bones of something not quite human and not quite ape out
of the Ethiopian dust. Taxonomists, the obsessive-compulsive scientists tasked with naming things, labeled her *Australopithecus
afarensis*. Someone with a little more imagination, however, called
her Lucy. With long arms and a small skull but the bones of a
bipedal walker, Lucy seemed like one of our links. By understanding her we might understand ourselves.

What was Lucy? Who was Lucy? Was she the connection
between beings more like us and those more like others? Other
questions occur to me, too: What was it like to discover her? How
did it feel to wipe away the dust? I suppose that looking into the
empty eye sockets of Lucy's reconstructed skull for the first time
was like looking into one's beginning, like seeing time rewind.

~

Over several evenings in 1977, I sat in front of the television with
the rest of my family, bubbling in a stew of emotions as the

fibrous and tangled roots of Alex Haley's ancestors came to life in a Technicolor glow. For those few days, I saw a different Africa than the one I'd been shown in the Tarzan movies and Compton's Encyclopedia. Watching *Roots* I realized that families and communities with rites and rituals weren't invented by white people. Early in the series, a strong black father held his infant son, Kunta Kinte, to the heavens: "Behold—the only thing greater than yourself!" Kunta had a place in the world, I understood, and—as the black baby boy wriggled in those big black hands under an inky African sky—I felt I did, too. I was part of something much greater. The next day I went to school prouder than ever to be in my brown skin. A black kid living in the boondocks of Edgefield, South Carolina, was descended from people like Kunta—strong, proud, and free. I wondered what tribe my ancestors had come from.

But as the nights of the program wore on, the pride grew more complex. Just as Kunta's life was unfolding into the promise of youth, everything changed. The slavers came, kidnapping and killing. Kunta was suddenly someone's property. Watching, I felt exposed. Sure, I had known what slavery was—and even that I was probably descended from enslaved Africans—but this was the first time it had been in my face so bluntly. Now, I thought, everyone knew. Painful scenes of separation, abduction, and enslavement were there for the world to see, on network television. My classmates and friends, most of whom were white, could now look right through my guise, back to the legacy of subjugation from whence I'd come.

Going to school after *Roots* was hard. I was shocked and ashamed at the betrayal that had been a part of sub-Saharan culture for centuries. I was embarrassed that Kunta Kinte's father and the strong warriors had not been able to fight off the slavers somehow. The torturous Middle Passage horrified me. In my mostly white classes, I felt even blacker. I wondered if people could see what I was feeling: anger, sadness, and shame. My white teachers and friends, however, didn't talk about the show at all. There were no class discussions. It was as if some taboo would be violated if anyone white said anything to anybody black about the truth. Stark history hurts sometimes.

Among the black kids it was different. They recast the characters I'd seen as strong as insults by calling others "Kunta," "Kizzy," or "Chicken George." It was meant to hurt and it did. To be recast as a slave by your own was a mind-blowing thing.

It was the first time I'd had to grapple with race in a significant way. The most racist slights I'd dealt with to that point often took form in people not anticipating or misunderstanding the differences that made me *me*. I'd learned quickly, for example, that the brittle plastic combs handed out on picture day weren't meant to groom tightly packed black-boy hair. When one of the combs broke off in my little Afro, classmates laughed. Afterward, I asked to wear my hair cut short so that grooming wasn't an issue. And for as long as I could remember others had observed that I "talked white." This somehow was supposed to make me better or smarter? For a few, it made me a "sellout," an Oreo—black on the outside and white within. But up to that point in my life, I hadn't yet taken a full-on gut punch of racism or truth and questioned my reality.

Roots set me—and the country—straight. On the nights when it aired everyone had gotten their chores and homework out of the way immediately. Mama had cooked dinner early and at eight o'clock we'd gathered around the four-legged Magnavox telebeast to see what the next episode held. No matter what my peers said, Kunta Kinte had been defiant in the face of his kidnapping and torturous journey to America. He'd refused to become someone he wasn't. The wise old slave Fiddler had shuffled along to get by because he didn't have a choice. Kunta's daughter, Kizzy, had gotten a little measure of revenge by sweetening a racist woman's water with her spit. His grandson, Chicken George, had played the system. The injustice that America was built on had been revealed in prime time. There was no sugarcoating, no Uncle Tomming, no romanticized good old days. *Roots* was the closest America had come since Martin Luther King Jr.'s death to having its nose forced in the unpleasant truth of a national shame.

The focus on their own American history brought genealogy to the attention of a black populace. Everyone suddenly began to want to know who they were. Despite my schoolyard ambivalence, I was no exception. Yoruba or Hausa—or maybe Fulani? Who are my people? Who am I?

The roots of most black folk in America were not nurtured but ripped violently from the ground in Mother Africa, bound and transplanted against our will. You will seldom hear about black Americans making pilgrimages to Ellis Island to bask in the glow of Lady Liberty's torch. Escape from religious or ethnic persecution is of course worthy of celebration. But the huddled masses below the decks of slave ships could only have wished for the opportunity to come here by choice.

The story of my paternal lineage, the one connected to the Home Place, is fragmented. It begins—to some extent—with Harry, a slave who came to Edgefield with his owners in 1790 or so. He is said to have been just a child then. How did he feel to move south? Who were the parents he left behind? Were they somewhere in the Middle Atlantic, where the white Lanhams had originally settled?

Was Harry alone in a new world, kept company by stained memories of a stinking slave hold and a family left behind on some distant shore, murdered in the Middle Passage, or ripped apart on an auction block? He lived to be sixty-three but there is no record of a marriage or any children. Who survived him? Was there a wife, sons, daughters?

The next pieces of the puzzle that I know of, Daddy Joe's parents—Abram and Louise—have never fit neatly into place. What link, how many generations connect Abram to Harry? With slave families so broken apart I can't say for certain.

There have been moments of enlightenment at family reunions and in stories of grandparents, aunts, uncles, and cousins. There was a time when family was close by. Before Daddy died, there were always summer gatherings at the Home Place. Cookouts were common, and my cousins from New York, Philadelphia, and other places up north would bring their sophisticated city selves down to the country to share in the modest bounty of our rural lives. Daddy grilled homegrown steaks and burgers on a cinder block barbecue pit. Mama cooked fresh vegetables from the garden and concocted desserts. There were always cakes, fruit cobblers, and pies. Sometimes, if we were willing to take our turns at the crank, homemade peach or strawberry ice cream topped off the feasts.

The adults sat around and talked. The Lanham siblings and a bunch of the cousins rode bikes, chased lightning bugs, and threw dirt clods at one another. Sometimes you could catch bits and pieces of the grown-up talk; new stresses, old times, dead relatives, and living ghosts filtered into our play. The names of our ancestors—Daddy Joe, Abram, Big Mama, Cousin Burl—peppered the conversations. Those times with my extended family helped me understand that beyond Edgefield and those firefly-filled July nights, I was a part of a community of people who knew and accepted me for who I was. Everyone was celebrated for something.

The love of family, food, conversations, and cousins was special. But as time passed, people died and the gatherings stopped. The family began to disintegrate.

⁓

My family tree's roots are withering. The black Lanham men connected to the Home Place are few in number. There are three of us left: me; my brother, Jock; and my son, Colby. We're a critically endangered species. And so with the ties fading and time running out—and for those who came before and those who might come after—I set out to dig deeper into who and what I am.

I remember Mamatha's obsession with digging. Her side yard never seemed to be what she wanted. Wild onions, dandelions, and an impressive assortment of weeds and grasses found good footing in the rich soil. Mamatha liked to garden in clean dirt and was none too thrilled with the constant botanical invasions. And so she went to war every spring, chopping and churning with a hoe every green thing that she had not planted there. I was often by her side, digging in what was only a temporary victory. The unwanted things always came back.

Ancestors are like those weeds; although the tops are chopped away, the twisting, turning roots may persist, hidden to grow again another season. Seed gets thrown to the wind, providing both truth and misinformation. I needed to plunge through the tangle.

The serious rooting really started one night in the early 1990s. Arriving home from a weekend away, I found a message waiting on the answering machine, from a man claiming to be one of the

"Kentucky Lanhams." He wanted to know about the Edgefield Lanhams. Up until that point I hadn't known that there *were* Lanhams in Kentucky—not black ones, anyway—and had the sneaking suspicion that he didn't know I was one of the darker-hued people carrying the surname. I returned the man's call the next day, and after some pleasant small talk, let him know that I was indeed Joseph Lanham. I also told him that I was a black man. After a pregnant pause, our conversation ended—politely, but abruptly. He promised to keep me in the Lanham loop, but I didn't expect to hear from him again and I didn't.

Although the call hadn't yielded the fruit the man thought it would, it spurred something in me. It was almost like hearing the sound of Mamatha's hoe slicing into weedy soil. Just as I couldn't lie idly by while she worked, I felt drawn in by the Kentucky man's dead-end call.

Sometime before this incident—a few months, maybe even a year or two—I'd dropped into the local pharmacy to pick up some photos I'd had developed. I'd collected an envelope with the name "Joseph Lanham" on it and gone on my way. But just outside the pharmacy door, I'd sneaked a peek at what were supposed to be pictures of a recent trip to the Colorado Rockies. Instead staring back at me had been the faces of white people I didn't know.

I had returned to the counter and quickly found out that the packet I had collected was for Joseph *W.* Lanham, not for me, Joseph *D.* Lanham. How interesting: there was more than one of me. But I hadn't dug any deeper into who the white Lanham, in the same town with almost the same name, was. I'd had other things going on: a new infant daughter, a stubborn dissertation, lots of bills, and not much money. So I'd filed the coincidence away in the back of my brain. But after the call from Kentucky, I reopened the file.

Aside from his white skin, Joseph W. Lanham was more like me than I ever would've imagined. A native of Edgefield and an entomology professor at Clemson, he had spent a great portion of his academic life toiling away with insects in the same building complex where I now spent my days thinking about songbirds and land ethic. Was he related to Billy Lanham, who lived just up the road from the Home Place? We had been on neighborly terms with him and his family, but there was always some kind of invisible barrier that kept us from fully socializing.

I dug a little deeper and discovered that the other Professor Lanham was in a retirement home. I called, but found out that he was very ill and unable to talk. The feeling of being so close to but so far from someone who not only shared a name but maybe some history with me was almost painful. I was less than ten miles and just a few minutes away from making a connection to the elusive roots so many seek. A week or so later Joseph W. Lanham was dead. I was crushed. There was a strong possibility that some of his ancestors had owned some of mine. But there would be no enlightening conversation; no nervous visitation; no heart-wrenching son-of-master, son-of-slave reconnection; no spell-binding reunion.

Unsure where to turn next, I dropped the Lanham name into what was then a new and magical thing—the Internet search engine. In the instantaneous miracle of the binary library, the Lanham name appeared. The online work was like digging a hole in the sand, though, your efforts constantly stymied by the dirt you removed spilling back in. I had to keep skimming past the oft-repeated material about white people and Harry, a slave who, the Internet said, loved his masters so much that he had decided to remain chattel property when offered freedom. I had my answer, supposedly, on how he'd felt leaving home: Harry was thrilled, happy, to follow and then stay. I had my doubts.

A pretty thorough effort had been made to compile the white Lanham history. From England, the white Lanhams had flowed into the Middle Atlantic and Maryland in the mid- to late 1700s. From there the Lanham tendrils grew westward into Kentucky and south into South Carolina and even Texas. There were connections to the Alamo, Confederate Civil War heroes—I hoped like hell there'd be no black Lanhams who showed up as Confederate soldiers—and the cotton gin, and accusations of assault and murder. But there was little said, good or bad, about anyone black.

Sometimes I found myself chopping hard, trying to separate the things I wanted to know from the things I didn't. There are aspirations we have for our ancestors. We hope we'll find heroes and proud people—fighters like Kunta Kinte, the Union soldiers who fought for the Massachusetts 54th, or the Tuskegee Airmen. No black person wants to find relatives who settled for captivity when they could have had freedom. I had to go beyond the "Happy Harry" story.

Word of mouth and some checking with Mama led me to the Tompkins Library, on the square in downtown Edgefield. Ever since *Roots* I had dreamed of making a pilgrimage of discovery. As I drove down Highway 25, through the wooded back stretches of Greenwood and finally into Edgefield, conversation with an older, wiser—and white—friend about family and connections made the two-plus-hour drive seem much shorter. Coleman Glaze had also heard of the little genealogy library and thought that perhaps he'd trace some of his own Edgefield lineage.

"C. O.," as his family calls him, was a visionary Lowcountry businessman who was among the first to integrate banks and stand

up for equal treatment of all Charleston's citizens. He "earned" the
esteemed title of "nigger lover" from townspeople and bore the
burden of humanitarianism with strength and grit. En route I
joked that perhaps his ancestors and mine had been business part-
ners, and that maybe it was time for me to collect on the overdue
salary. He assured me that his poor Scots-Irish ancestors, who at
times had worked shoulder to shoulder with black folks building portions of Charleston, didn't own my relatives or any other
people for that matter.

I read a sign aloud to Coleman as we entered the square: "We
lynch." The sign—"W. E. Lynch & Co."—is all that is left of a general
merchandise and clothing store in "uptown" Edgefield. It probably
used to represent the true sentiments of more than a few of the
town's historic personalities, including the ten governors Edgefield
has produced. The quiet nature of the town belies its often-violent
history; hatred festers just under the skin of the place. It seethes
and foams, sometimes oozing out even now.

The Tompkins Library sits a couple of doors down the street
from Lynch's. The building that is now roots central for Edgefield
County and the old Ninety Six District is also where I used to
search for bird books. I had racked up some serious fines because
I couldn't let books like *Fifty Birds of Town and City* go back on
time. Now, some thirty years later, I was back—and a little nervous
that an overdue alarm would go off when I crossed the threshold.

The library's interior was unremarkable, with the exception of
a display of clay jugs made by some of Edgefield's famous slave pot-
ters. The docent, Tanya, greeted us as we entered. I'd called earlier;
the mere mention of the Lanham name made her perk up.

"Yes, I know the Lanham family and the Harry story very well,"
Tanya said. She retreated to her desk and pulled out a copy of

Home Place: The Journal of the Old Ninety Six African American Genealogical Society. Inside was a familiar story: "Sacred to the Memory of Harry." It was nothing new but I was impressed that there was a society dedicated to black history in Edgefield.

Tanya turned a couple of pages in another volume. She'd been studying and documenting black cemeteries in Edgefield. A priority among her projects was identifying Harry's grave. "I'd love to have you come back when it's colder and help me look for it," she said. "Then we won't have to worry as much about snakes, but we'll have to look out for the deer hunters. I'm pretty sure we found it but I'd like to get closer to it to make sure and gather some more data for my project."

This was much more than I had expected. Seeing Harry Lanham's grave would finally provide a tangible link to my family's taproot. Here was proof that the man had actually existed, a near guarantee that the deepest connection to my Home Place legacy lies buried in the woods, still giving to the land on which he toiled. His master now isn't men, but the recovering forest.

We talked about the possibilities for an expedition and the Lanham legacy, both black and white. A volunteer who'd been toiling in the back room came out. There was excitement. Almost as an afterthought, Tanya asked me if I'd heard of the *Wanderer*. Pulling some documents from her desk, she showed me a well-worn copy of a 1908 article entitled "Survivors from the Cargo of the Slave Yacht *Wanderer*." The piece was about a converted yacht that had delivered an illegal cargo of African slaves in 1858, almost fifty years after such importations were banned. Knowing their cargo would be seized if discovered, the ship's crew had ported at Jekyll Island, off the Georgia coast, and quickly dispersed many of its surviving captives to buyers in Florida, Georgia, and South

Carolina. A group of about two hundred people were ferried up the Savannah River to Augusta, Georgia, and a few eventually to Edgefield.

"Apparently some of these slaves were purchased by the Lanham estate," Tanya said. She flipped through another page or two and stopped at a plate labeled "Survivors of the Slave Ship *Wanderer*," neatly partitioned into four panes. Four black faces stared at me from the grainy two-tone photocopy. There were two names each for three of them—the real ones they had brought from Africa and the "Toby" names they'd been given as slaves.

In the upper left, exhibit (*a*): Zow Uncola (Tom Johnson), a middle-aged, coal-skinned man wearing a wrinkled work shirt and suspenders, and standing in front of a tree with furrowed bark. He looked almost happy, but tired. I wondered if he remembered what any of the trees from Africa looked like.

In the upper right, exhibit (*b*): Manchuella (Katie Noble). With poorly fitting wire-rimmed glasses and a white scarf covering her head, she looked to be in her late fifties or even older. Maybe the patterned dress, beaded necklace, and hoop earrings spoke to individuality in a world that limited her humanity by race and gender. The article said that many of the *Wanderer*'s captives were partial to red. I wondered if the color suited her.

In the lower left, exhibit (*c*): Mabiala (Uster Williams), grizzled and maybe confused, his eyes narrowed to slits. Mabiala, according to the article, was blind and believed that his afflictions were the result of witchcraft. Did he think that his capture and servitude were the product of the same malevolent spirit? Did the new and "better" god his masters gave him deliver him from his afflictions?

And in the lower right frame I discovered my Lucy. But this was not Olduvai Gorge or Ethiopia; it was Edgefield, South Carolina.

Staring out from the paper, with familiar eyes and a scarf-wrapped head, was a dark-skinned woman with a slight smile. Her hair, like Manchuella's, was hidden by a white rag, and she wore a similar checkered dress but without necklace or earrings. Unlike Manchuella, however, she had just one name: Lucy Lanham.

I was stunned. Looking back from the page was a woman more African than American, with my last name. And she had been among the last human chattel to enter the country. I had to sit down. I hadn't prepared for the rush of emotion I was experiencing. I felt everything at the same time: joy, pain, anger, sadness, surprise, pride. I wanted to laugh, cry, shout to someone that maybe I'd found a part of me! Tanya gave me a much-needed pause, then told me the rest of the story.

The new Africans had caused a stir among the established slave community. After all, new people fresh out of Africa were uncommon by that time. Perhaps some of the older slaves were reminded of their own connections to and severance from different, freer lives. Furthermore, the captives had been taken from the Congo, a region off the normal slave trade track. Even in 1908, when the article had been written, some of the former slaves retained portions of their birth language and remembered landscapes and sunsets. Tanya said that some of the slaves were even taken to Columbia, the capital, to be put on display for their novel ways and appearance—treated as livestock and not human beings.

Looking into Lucy's face, I wondered if she had been one of the people who made me who I am. She'd been just three years old when she was taken captive on the *Wanderer*. Even after emancipation, Lucy and the other woman in the photo, Katie Noble, were still captives of an oppressive system. She was listed as living on the plantation of Senator Benjamin Tillman—a hateful, racist man, who previously, as governor, had sanctioned terrorism against black people and earned the nickname "Pitchfork Ben." One can only imagine that life under Tillman's bigoted thumb was probably not much better than being a slave.

Former slaves who remained employees of the landed gentry were often doomed to life as tenant farmers. Although sharecroppers were physically free of shackles and chains, they still found themselves bound by Jim Crow and a never-ending cycle of debt and work that could only be paid by borrowing more and falling deeper into debt. Segregation and lack of access to anything near equal was just life. Suddenly I realized that I did have heroes in my family: the survivors who had lived through the most inhumane conditions and had yet produced farmers and teachers and college professors. Institutionalized financial insolvency and intolerance kept a lot of black people down. My relatives somehow rose above it, even in the shadow of someone as purely evil as Benjamin Tillman.

The irony of Lucy's connection to Pitchfork Ben is that my life is tied up in his legacy, too. One day my daughter, Alexis, then a sophomore at Clemson, was enjoying a sunny respite between classes in the Carillon Garden, a little memorial park that lies in the shadow of the iconic Tillman Hall. She called me. "Daddy, I'm sitting here and I looked down and there is a memorial brick with the name Benjamin Tillman Lanham on it. Who is he?" she asked. I wasn't sure, but I told her about the history, that the Tillmans and Lanhams were both out of Edgefield. She was surprised to hear that she was possibly connected to Clemson by more than just her parents' alumni statuses and a degree she was working toward. I suppose breaking away from the plantation legacy is not easy.

The connections to the other Joseph Lanham, to Ben Tillman, and to my alma mater—"Where the Blue Ridge yawns its greatness"—

gnaw at me. As fervently as I adore the burnt orange and northwest purple of my school, the realization that I studied and still work within the confines of a slaveholding legacy is sobering. The university's links to people like John C. Calhoun, an unwavering advocate of slavery and early proponent of secession; Thomas Green Clemson, a slave owner; Pitchfork Ben; and Strom Thurmond, a segregationist hypocrite who didn't mind race mixing at very intimate levels, is no cause for pride. Fortunately history can be redeemed by the passage of time, circumstance, and people courageous enough to change things.

I lingered in the Tompkins Library for a while longer that afternoon, but with the emotional toll of all the discovery and time traveling there wasn't much more I could assimilate. Tanya gave me some additional genealogy pointers and warned me that although the connections between my life and the *Wanderer* were appealing, there might not have been blood ties.

After all, Lucy had been a young girl when Harry was an old man. He might even have been dead by the time she appeared. So, I wondered, was I a descendant of Harry, Lucy, both, or neither? Did anything more than coincidence find Lucy in the same time, place, and circumstances as Harry? Could my great-grandmother Louise have in fact been Lucy? And in the grand scheme of things, did the hard facts truly matter? Were Harry and Lucy both family simply by virtue of shared experience with my ancestors, whoever they were?

Later I would have one last avenue of research open to me. There are tools now, even greater than the magic of the Internet, to help me get closer to answers. Geneticists have figured out how to take the elemental pieces of me—or anyone else—compare it to the DNA of people in places like West Africa or the Congo or Great Britain, and tell me if we might share a limb on the human family tree. I suppose it's my grandmother's digging genes—an overdose of natural curiosity—and my own background as a trained scientist that inspired me to want to know even more about who I am. I ordered two genetic tests, one that promised to illuminate my African ancestry and another that would go even further to fill in the genetic gaps. A sample of saliva and six weeks might give me answers to questions that many have had to work for decades or longer to attain.

And so I sent spit and waited.

I didn't open the first envelope the day I got it. Instead I put it aside, as if it were some past-due bill. A week later, I broke the glued seal.

In front of me lay my lineage. Eighty percent of who I am grows from thickly matted roots in west and central Africa. Mama's line sprouts from Sierra Leone and the Mende people, Daddy's line from Cameroon and the Bamileke. My mother's roots share the same soil as Cinque and the Mende warriors who took their liberty by force on the slave ship *Amistad*. Her years at Talladega, in the presence of the murals depicting the mutiny, seemed fated in retrospect. My father comes from people famed for farming around chiefdoms. That some called Daddy "Big Chief"—and that he worked hardest farming and caring for the land—seems appropriate. And it was worth noting that Lucy and Daddy shared a central Africa geographical connection. The links between us couldn't be definitively determined, but the possibility remained. That was the critical thing, for me. Archeology is a never-ending dig and puzzle-solving game.

What about the other portion of the buried root? When the next envelope arrived I didn't delay. I ripped the envelope open to find Irish, British, and German rootlets, along with expanded growth into Scandinavia, a smidge of American Indian, a hint of southeast Asian, and a drop of Neanderthal.

That I'm mixed up genetically is no real surprise. We're all mostly mutts, amalgamations of movements, migrations, causes, and circumstances. But I'm a black American and proudly so. History is the glue that brings my roots together, and it rends them apart as well.

Family Reunion

To the memory of
HARRY
He was born in Maryland in the year 1787
And he died on the 26th day of November
In 1860, at the residence of his master
Josias Lanham
Edgefield District, S.C.
He emigrated to the District with
His master in
Early youth and continued
True and faithful
To the end of his life
He was worthy of and possessed
The confidence of his master

— Joseph Lanham,
"Sacred to the Memory of Harry"[1]

ONE DAY I DECIDED TO VISIT MY EXTENDED "FAMILY" AT
Republican Baptist Church. The church shared the same non-
descript and bumpy stretch of country road as the Home Place,
but I had never been there before. On our daring extended bicycle
forays as children, Bug and I had caught occasional glimpses of the
white building glowing at the end of Republican Road. Ultimately,
however, it was mysterious, off limits.

The little country church shimmered in the afternoon swelter.

---

1. *FGCGS Bulletin* 22, no. 8 (April 1991). Like so many of the details around Harry's life, the dates of his birth and death are difficult to verify.

Nestled among the fading green of late August, the crisp, clean Southern Baptist angles cut through the heavy haze. It was an eerily quiet scene. With the heat and humidity needle winding toward the hellish mark, only a persistent red-eyed vireo and stubborn indigo bunting were still singing. The silence enhanced the surrealism. The pale worship house floated like a mirage on a pond of gummy black asphalt.

I had come searching for long-lost family, following Tanya's leads. My link to all things "Lanham, Harry," she revealed, had supposedly been buried here. Allegedly a gesture of gratitude and respect from his "kind" master, Harry's interment among the Lanhams kept him bound to his white owners even unto death.

Had this been a Sunday, a worship day, I would not have made the pilgrimage. Republican Baptist's congregation is lily white. As is the case across so much of the South, God usually sees congregations in separate but equal reverence. While I thought my "could-be" patriarch would have been happy to know I was there, the welcome from the other Lanhams, in both the congregation and the graveyard, might have been more questionable. Most of the deceased family I had dropped in on would no sooner have had me over for dinner as called me cousin.

I tried to shake off my uneasiness. Surely visiting a loved one's resting place would be viewed sympathetically by anyone. But there was still dread. Maybe it was the stillness, the heaviness of the afternoon and the gathering thunderheads. Or maybe it was the rows of miniature Confederate battle flags, little postcard-sized pieces of scarlet crossed with blue bars and white stars coming to occasional life in the slightest breeze. Were the dead watching me?

But the draw of connecting, of pulling the ends of my family circle closed, was irresistible. And so I lifted the latch of the woven-aluminum gate standing between me and the possibility of knowing something more.

⁓

Lanham is an old English surname. It's uncommon enough that reinforcing its pronunciation—"Lan-um"—and spelling—L – A – N ("n" as in "no") – H – A – M ("m" as in "Mary")—has become routine. But there I was, surrounded by the familiar two syllables. I could see them everywhere, etched deeply into granite monoliths and modest marble tablets. I'd never seen the name so many times in one place: for a moment I was oddly comforted, almost peacefully reflective, inexplicably proud. So many buried here sharing my last name seemed to confirm that this place was—is—somehow central to who I am. But the scarlet banners of the Confederacy quickly brought me to my senses. I'm a different kind of Lanham.

My search took me past hero after hero, fallen soldiers from the "War of Secession" who fought for a cause they no doubt believed just. Heroes who claimed the right to independence and self-determination while denying others the same. "Hero"—in retrospect—wouldn't be the term I would choose. I covered ground speedily. Though the cemetery was small, with few rows to trod, I found no stone marking the grave of Harry Lanham.

That genealogical society bulletin—the one that pays homage to Harry—paints a picture of blissful bondage and traces Harry's happy "emigration" from Maryland to Edgefield with his "friends," to try cotton as a new and exciting venture. It seems like such a happy time! Three chums headed off on an adventure that would make cotton king!

Try this approach instead. Imagine being taken away from your family and friends. They're the people you've known all of your life. They're the people who know *you* best. Their companionship was base compensation for bondage. But then one day you are told that you're leaving them behind to chop and bale cotton instead of cutting and hanging tobacco. That a teenager happily abandoned the familiar is beyond belief. But the bulletin said it was so, in plain black and white. And here I was—black in the midst of lots of white.

Did Harry look for his reward in heaven? Did he hope for one last freedom, to lie where he chose and spend an eternity moldering among his own? Being buried with one's owner—the fellow human being who could say "come or go," "worship or work," "live or die"—might not have been what he envisioned for an afterlife free of chains. As I made the rounds and the sweat poured, as the cicadas droned and the indigo bunting songs rolled, there was still no sign of Harry's last reward.

The dead aren't usually so elusive. My more recent ancestors lie just a few miles from Republican Baptist. I can envision Jeter Baptist Church on its own island of blacktop, nestled in the same sea of oak, pine, and hickory. My Jeter family rests behind the remodeled building, once peeling wooden clapboard, now red brick and mortar. The lines, though also Baptist, are a little less crisp than Republican's. There are few "extras" at Jeter: no colorful new playground, no well-built family-life center, no spacious meeting halls. It's just a church in the woods.

Offering plates probably clink a little more at Jeter than at Republican, where more of the money folds and lands softly, with a dead president looking up at you. The Jeter lawn needs no maintenance; red clay and asphalt require little in the way of mowing. There are no neat sidewalks or well-tended shrubbery. No fence guards the resting place of a family who would not question my visit. At Jeter I would be welcomed by the souls of the folks lying beneath my feet. The black Lanhams, my blood kin for sure—Joseph Samuel, Ethel, Louise, Abram, Pearl, Weesie—are all there. There are no flags to honor commitment to a lost cause, just fading, cheap plastic flowers scattered among listing monuments, weeds and saplings scouting the advance of the ever-encroaching forest. At Jeter, my family rests among tufts of broom sedge and tangles of briars, an interment reflective of hardscrabble lives protected by little and with final allegiance only to the clayey soil they worked.

The similarities and razor-sharp distinctions between the two places—both committed to God, salvation, and, to a large extent, the Lanham name—illustrate the chasms and closeness in a culture that so defined a time, place, and way of life. The differences were made clear and similarities suppressed to keep things separate and unequal.

The sweat flowed down my face, dripping to water the green carpet of the Republican cemetery. Some justice and long-overdue homage to the blood and tears of a man named Harry, I thought. Both satisfied and not, I decided to leave the place to the buntings and building clouds. It was hot and I'd dutifully searched for an end and a beginning.

As I left, I knelt beside a monument erected decades ago to some pale-complexioned "cousin." Embracing the corner of his tombstone in a familial embrace, as if it were a shoulder, and giving my best ear-to-ear, thirty-two-tooth salute, I snapped a selfie of our Republican Road reunion. The star-crossed flag of history and hate waved languidly between us. I felt hot as hell but alive in the late-afternoon sun. The other Lanhams in my company were cold as stone, though I didn't proffer a guess as to whether or not their new home was warmer than mine. I was glad I hadn't found Harry lying among them.

Patchwork Legacy

"Hope" is the thing with feathers—
That perches in the soul—
And sings the tune without the words—
And never stops—at all.

⌐ Emily Dickinson

My Home Place inheritance is fractured now. It's a mere fragment of what it once was. Maybe it's best remembered fondly, in past tenses and better times. When I do visit the remnant we still own, I come away with a gnarled finger pointed squarely at those I blame for the loss.

Daddy's death came quickly and unexpectedly. The greed and lack of civility that followed were just as quick and perhaps even more unexpected. I remember the back and forth with a lawyer and discussions with aunts and uncles I once revered turning into nasty arguments. Even Mamatha seemed resigned to letting things go the wrong way. She sat by silently—tight lipped, with hands folded on her lap—as the land was torn apart by eyes turned toward quick cash. Mama was given little choice of what land we would retain by those who supposedly had our best interests at heart. Instead of a land legacy we got the leftovers.

The abandoned Ranch is decaying from the inside out. Beyond the faded brick facade things are falling apart, floors caving in and ceilings sagging. Attempts at keeping things together with a series of renters failed miserably. They had no investment in or connection to the place beyond the next month's rent and so they abused the privilege of staying there. Mamatha's Ramshackle is disappearing quickly, too. The barn was consumed by pine, whippy saplings, and briars long ago. Somehow the smokehouse is still standing. Pickers have looted the house. I visited a while ago and found a pile of old letters, books, and rifled-through trash dumped on the back porch. There was treasure in the refuse, though, including a Farm Service record book from 1934 that showed Daddy Joe's plans for planting and pasturage. I cautiously walked through the house, expecting at any moment to either fall through the floor or have the ceiling collapse on me. The risk was worth it. I found a bag of scrap-cloth pieces that Mamatha had probably been collecting for a patchwork quilt. I gathered up what I could and left the place that had nurtured me with bits and pieces of my history. All along, I didn't feel alone. It was as if some kind presence ushered me through a place I needed to be one last time. Those remnants, seven acres, and mostly good memories are all I have left now. It's my patchwork legacy.

Daddy's death was like a terminal diagnosis for the Home Place. Jock hangs on to his home on the first terrace and his presence is a sort of life support that keeps the thing breathing in shallow, struggling gasps. I'm not overly optimistic that the happy Home Place of my childhood will ever be anything more than a good story gone sad. It's a hard truth that's settled in over the years. Mentally I'm moving on.

So then where do my hopes lie? They are still landbound. Mama's Ninety Six Home Place also has a long legacy and though some of that land has been lost, too, much of it still resides in Jones-family ownership—more than 120 acres of piedmont slate-belt woodland just begging for love and attention.

I came to know the Ninety Six Home Place late. Although I visited it a couple of times as a child, there was no real connection there for me. I never met Mama's parents, Granddaddy Jim and Grandma Julia. Both died before I was born. Behind them they left land. Mama and Daddy traveled there from time to time and even replanted pines after some of the timber was logged decades ago. When I was working on my doctorate, in the early 1990s, Mama wanted to sell timber and understand how she might keep the trees growing and the cash from them flowing. With Aldo Leopold's revival of his beloved farm and *A Sand County Almanac*'s words winding through my head, I began to think about that land in a different way. Maybe I could make the Ninety Six Home Place into something special, a working refuge where wild things were the priority and where artful management might make a positive difference.

Losing the Edgefield land and most of the legacy that went along with it shook me into a new reality and ignited a rapidly expanding appreciation for Ninety Six. Because I didn't grow up there, though, I've had to learn to love the place. It has another feel. Maybe it's the way the land lies on different rock, which makes parts of it want to be piedmont prairie. Maybe it's how the loblollies grow tallest on the east side. Maybe it's the little patch of loamy, mossy high ground where the red cedar, post oak, and persimmons grow and the bucks like to rub and roam. Maybe it's the way the little no-name creek creeps through the dark, narrow bottom, nourishing the sycamores, hackberries, and ironwood. Maybe it's the hardwood slope to the west, where the white oaks throw acorns to the wildlings every couple of years and the ovenbirds sing in spring. There's a different rhythm to the place that I want to hold onto. It's a chance at reviving legacy.

Greed was the cancer that killed the Lanham Edgefield legacy.

There were no plans made for anything other than getting and spending. But in practicing a land ethic Aldo Leopold suggested that we thoughtfully tinker and mindfully keep all the parts. Being entrusted with the stewardship of the Ninety Six acres is a special thing. As I've grown closer to the Ninety Six I've begun to loosen my grip on the Edgefield kingdom. It will always be home but my seven acres often seem a million miles away. The memories are close by, though, and I can visit them anytime.

The decisions to come on the newfound legacy are myriad. When's the next cut? Should I row thin, cut selectively, or clear-cut a small patch? The little prairie remnant and bobwhite covey are struggling and demand fire if they're to thrive. Do I farm for wildlife? Should I tend turnips and clover for the deer and hedges of Chickasaw plums for the yellow-breasted chats? Perhaps I'll punch a well and build a little cabin in the Ninety Six woods. Maybe I'll sit on the porch and watch the sun set behind the tall pines and let the whip-poor-wills whine me to sleep. Maybe I'll write about it.

Trying to do what's best by nature is a guessing game with long-term stakes. Good decisions mean that the soil and water will prosper. The trees will prosper. The wild things will prosper. In that natural prospering all of us will become wealthier in richer dawn choruses and endless golden sunsets. The investment is called legacy. If I can see, feel, touch, and smell these things once more on a piece of land I can call my own, I'll be home again.

So maybe there's still hope. Home, after all, is more than a place on a map. It's a place in the heart.

Acknowledgments

THIS WORK IS FOR THE LAND THAT NURTURES ME. IT IS AN homage to a place that created confidence and comfort. It is a work of gratitude written to those wondering wanderers who stoke my heart's fire. It is a testament to the wild things and places that inspire me. It is an acknowledgment of love to all who've made this story possible.

Beyond abundant thanks, I am grateful—

FOR Ms. Beasley, Marion Marshall Gary, Jim Schindler, Patty Gowaty, Sid Gauthreaux, Dave Guynn, Tom Waldrop, and Pat Layton—identity facilitators from the second grade through graduate school and my early professional fledging, who simply let the nature in me flow through. Each of you opened a portal that helped make my dreams and this work a reality.

FOR Craftsbury Common, Vermont, and the Wildbranch Writing Workshop—a faraway place and an unexpected opportunity that made deep thinking about my South Carolina home possible.

FOR Janisse Ray, for early inspiration and showing me that a love for southern land and a heartfelt appreciation for nature and family were worth sharing. You saw promise first and for that I will always be grateful.

FOR Joel Vance, who became my fast friend and encouraged an expansion of my range into the realm of outdoor writing, fostering early confidence as I worked to gain my writing sea legs.

FOR Jennifer Sahn and Emerson "Chip" Blake at *Orion*, for granting precious print space, publishing an early essay ("Hope and Feathers") that gave me critical traction in the community, and making connections to other writers that still buoy me.

FOR soulful exchanges on warm Craftsbury Common evenings with Kate Johnson, Tovar Cerulli, Doug Johnson, and Anne Bemis Day, who bolstered the writing spirit and offered instant acceptance.

FOR John Lane, poet laureate of the southern piedmont and anthropocene disciple, who has been a major force in my writing evolution. His friendship and encouragement to "keep the strength in your sword arm" has been, time and time again, a gently powerful force in my work. I'm grateful, as well, to Betsy Teter at Hub City Press and to Dorinda Dallmeyer for urging my creative momentum forward with opportunities to share my work in sundry ways before this book was done. Thanks will never be enough.

FOR Camille Dungy and Lauret Savoy, rare nature-writing birds of color, who are exemplars of art and excellence in the craft, moving minds and hearts toward nature through differently hued lenses, and who provided friendship, support, and sustaining advice.

FOR Milkweed Editions, where Daniel Slager and Patrick Thomas rolled the dice on a woefully thin manuscript from an unproven novice. Thank you for the opportunity to put my heart on your paper. It has been a winding and sometimes hilly journey but you insisted all along that the hard walk would be worth the effort. Thank you for your patience during the times when I wondered if the trail would ever end. A special debt is owed to my anchor editor, Joey McGarvey, who in the last legs of the journey artfully shaped a lifetime of memories and eight-plus years' worth of writing into a better story and restored failing confidence.

FOR the kind souls, special places, and moments that formed this story along the way—long before and up to now—a flocking, flowing murmuration of beloved kindred spirits, who have given time, effort, and inspiration. Find yourself tucked tight between the lines and tangled in the words. Wander within them. Linger on the edges of what you think I meant to say. Rest in the shade of the shared sweet spots and remember fondly when the wood thrush sings at dawn or swans call in the night. Know that you've been a part of a story still being written. Thank you.

FOR my family—my wife, Janice Garrison Lanham; our children, Alexis and Colby—your support through decades of a personal evolution brings me to this point of reckoning with who I am going forward. Thank you for unconditional acceptance and for being patient with the persistent imperfectionist I work hard at being.

FOR my Home Place family foundation—Mama and Daddy, Willie May Jones and the late James Hoover—so much is owed to you both. Most of what I can remember now from way too many years ago was written here in hopes of honoring the upbringing you worked hard to make happen, in the best ways you knew how. Thank you, Daddy Joe, for your courage to lead Lanhams through the toughest of times, willing us all a land legacy worth remembering and passing on to me your name and the strength to tell the story as best I could. And to Mamatha, who said that one day my story—the good and the bad—would be written across the heavens for all to see, thank you for the gift of sight. In recalling what my life has been, seeing what it is, and dreaming of what it might be, you were at the root of the twining vine.

FOR Jock, Julia, and Jennifer, thank you for the rich palette of closest kinship. We've all meandered back and forth, braided sibling streams in touch and then not, but always of the same headwaters born. I hope my recollections ring true and bring more smiles than otherwise in your remembering and more time together for all of us.

AND, FINALLY, FOR a line of unnamed ancestors, to whom I owe life itself. They had no choice in working the land, but from bondaged toil and constant struggle made a future possible in which I could freely choose the land as my first and everlasting love.

Affection is the tie that binds all of this together.

Love,
Drew

D. Colby Lanham

J. DREW LANHAM is a native of Edgefield, South Carolina, and an Alumni Distinguished Professor of Wildlife Ecology and Master Teacher at Clemson University. Lanham is a birder, naturalist, and hunter-conservationist who has published essays and poetry in publications including *Orion*, *Flycatcher*, and *Wilderness*, and in several anthologies, including *The Colors of Nature*, *State of the Heart*, *Bartram's Living Legacy*, and *Carolina Writers at Home*, among others. He and his family live in the Upstate of South Carolina, a soaring hawk's downhill glide from the southern Appalachian escarpment that the Cherokee once called the Blue Wall.

The Editor's Circle of Milkweed Editions

We gratefully acknowledge the following individuals
for their leadership support of the literary arts.

∼

Interior design by Connie Kuhnz
Typeset in Minion Pro
by Bookmobile Design and Digital Publisher Services

Designed by Robert Slimbach in 1990 for Adobe Systems, Minion was inspired by late Renaissance-era type. Slimbach described it as having "a simplified structure and moderate proportions" that make it ideal for use in books.

MAP OF FARM

4

Draw in the outline of the farm or farms.
Locate the roads, buildings, fences, woods, and any other fixed points.
Draw in the crop boundaries as land is used in the present crop year.
Letter the crop fields *A, B*, etc., and transfer to next page for crop record.

WOODS

12A
FA

3A F-B

2A FE
1A FC
1A F-D
WOODS

WOODS

IDLE

FF

3A

6A
IDLE

2A F-G

3A F-H

3A F-I
2A F-J

1A IDLE
3A IDLE

PASTURE